# OUT

# OF

# EGYPT

## THE

## CLINTON DUKES

## STORY

**OUT OF EGYPT**



Published by Ascension Publishing, LLC

Ordering Information:

Quantity sales. Special discounts are available on quantity purchases by corporations, associations, and others. Orders made by U.S. trade bookstores and wholesalers, please contact the publisher or author at the telephone numbers or email addresses below:
804-464-8479/ 804-420-2135
AscensionPublishing@outlook.com
Authorclintodukesjr@gmail.com

Cover Illustration Copyright©

Cover Design by Cheryl Howard

Editing by Christopher L. Allen



Library of Congress Catalog Number: 2020904338

ISBN: 978-0-578-65748-6

1. Self Help 2. Biography

PRINTED IN THE UNITED STATES OF AMERICA

# FOREWORD

People always ask me why I say, "*Stay out of Egypt*." The phrase is not an attack on Egyptian people, history, culture, or society, but rather it is a reference to the biblical story found in the book of Exodus. The story talks about how the children of Israel were in hard bondage to the Egyptians for hundreds of years, and how living in such bondage affected every area of their lives. There can be many *Egypts* in our lives such as drugs, alcohol, sex, and money, etc. Anything that can hold us in bondage can be an *Egypt*. In this book, you will see how there have been many *Egypts* in my life and how I was able to obtain freedom from them and the process that I live by now to keep from being in bondage again. This is not a religious book, but God has definitely played a major role in my life and still does to this day. I hope that this book will simply inspire someone to know that regardless of the harmful decisions one has made in the past it doesn't have to define them for the rest of their lives. This is my story! A story of a young man growing, facing his fears, and healing every day. I have found out and decided that there is no need to return to *Egypt*. Whether I go or not, freedom is a better choice, but freedom is not free. It takes discipline and sacrifice to "*Stay out of Egypt" yall.*

# CONTENTS

# HOME

I was born on May 12, 1966, Clinton Hubert Dukes, Jr., (Tubby was my nickname) in Norfolk, Virginia, but raised in its sister city of Portsmouth. Portsmouth is a small-town rich in confederate, military, revolutionary and civil rights history. My earliest thoughts go back to a community called Cavalier Manor. For me, there has always been great pride associated with having been raised there. The *Manor* as it is so affectionately called was at one time the largest middle-class black community on the east coast. In the section that I lived in the streets were named after famous African Americans like Mineo Lane, Ellington Square, Horn Avenue, and Ekstine Drive. I didn't realize this until I was older and became somewhat conscious of my history. To be honest, it felt like you were better than the downtown blacks, because you weren't in the projects and the houses were newer. Even some of your neighbors would put their noses in the air to you. This place was home, and no one could tell me even to this day that the *Manor* wasn't the shit. Although I lived in a beautiful community, there wasn't much beauty in my home. I was born to two North Carolina natives, Clinton Dukes of Ahoskie, North Carolina and Aretha Lee Hall of Moyock, North Carolina.

I was more acquainted with my mother's side of the family. It seemed that they were always present. I didn't know much about my father's side of the family and he didn't talk much about his past. All I remembered was Uncle Paul, Grandma Jesse and my Aunt Joyce who was actually my cousin. She had a son named Tim Tim. He and I were close when we were younger, but our paths took us in different directions. My Aunt Joyce recently told me that my father added an "S" to his name, because their last name is Duke. I wondered what was going on in my father's head to make him want to change his name like that. I think that mystery was a part of the pain that he was in.

My father worked at the Norfolk Naval Base as a Cabinet Maker and my mother was a Homemaker. To my recollection, we never had a car and my mother, and I walked everywhere. She was affectionately known as Miss Rita to all my friends, because we would always play and hangout at my house. I was the only child, but

I was blessed to grow up with a great group of friends named Bud, Champ, Wayne, Grady, Oliver, Phillip, Troy, Vernon, Keith, Joe, and Rob J (R.I.P. Wayne and Rob). I needed them to because when I was out with them, I was at peace. When I went into the house it was another story, especially if my father had been drinking. My father was a cool man. He worked, gardened, and made the funniest jokes, but when he started drinking it was like a monster would come out. He would violently beat my mother and it would be no surprise to see my father chasing my mother down the street while I was out playing with my friends. I never knew or even asked my friends how they felt, or how did they processed what they were seeing. It was a part of my life growing up in the *Manor*. I hated my father because he would always build me up and then destroy me with his violent behavior. I recall one night I was in the bed and I awakened by a flash of light that ran through the hallway. As I arose out of my bed, I could hear the screams of a grown man coming from outside of the house. When I ran to see what had happened, I saw that my father had been set ablaze. He set himself on fire by falling asleep drunk with a cigarette in his hand. My father had 3rd-degree burns and was forced to retire. Alcohol had taken my father's job and his skin. My mother and father never slept in the same bed as far back as I can remember, so I never really saw how a married couple should function in happiness and peace. Although he never put a hand on me, the abuse that was displayed on my mother left a scar in me that can never be removed. My mother was my angel. She spoiled me and took me with her everywhere. I can still hear her saying, "Run Tubby run," when I was playing sports. I was so horrible at sports. I don't know why I was so bad at certain sports. Maybe it was because I was so incredibly skinny. People wondered why my nickname was Tubby. Well, it was told to me that when I was a baby, I was so fat that my parents called me Chubby, but Tubby stuck. As I grew older, I developed asthma and lost a lot a weight, but the nicknamed stayed. So now you have a skinny kid named Tubby. One thing that my mother made sure that I did was go to church. We went to New Bethel Baptist Church. It was in the center of the *Manor* and a place where I developed most of my very weak social skills. I was in the choir, played the drums, and ushered. I was also in the Boy Scouts. There was something about church that just stuck in my soul. In my opinion, we had the best choir in the land and the prettiest girls thanks to Karen and Katrina. It was a family environment and with every family we had our own set of issues. One of the things that church helped to bring out of me was my love for music. I was able to hear the instruments in every song and mimic the sounds of the singers. I wasn't a good singer, but I was able to imitate their sounds. I never shared this with many people, but the music kept me sane. It all started when I was outside playing with my friends and my friend Phillip gave me a double cassette of Prince to listen to. I believe it was the Controversy and Dirty Mind albums together. That music changed my life. With all the abuse and turmoil going on in my life I could turn this on and escape. Prince was bold, crazy, strange, gifted, talented, talked about and shunned, but he would not be denied. I wanted to be Prince. In fact, I was Prince. I recall the time when all my friends were outside playing, and I had the bright idea to dress up as Prince from the Dirty Mind album. Yes, I had on the trench coat, a bandana around my neck, black bikini briefs with the long thigh high stockings, and boots. I went to my front porch with my boom box and blasted the radio to *Uptown*, with full lip-sync and dance routine. You should have seen the looks on the faces of my friends. I have never been able to live that down. To this day, Prince remains to be the greatest artist ever put on this planet.

As far back as I can remember, I have always loved the ladies, and the *Manor* had plenty. I can remember names like Sheila, Karen, Tasha, Kim, and Tammy Lou. They were the young boys' dreams and desires. Some became like sisters, and others just remained lodged in a young boy's dreams. This one little girl whose name was Sherry, lived on Dandridge Drive, was so beautiful to me. She had the longest, and prettiest hair ever. She was very small and older than me. I never uttered a word to her, but I would see her sitting on the porch from time to time. She was so beautiful that I didn't think she was real. I believed there was no chance for a little skinny kid to gain her attention, so she just became another fantasy. The whole time I lived in the *Manor* I never told her. I should have, but life goes on and fear won the battle at that time. Now there were many more, but we don't have time or enough ink to put all my fantasy list on paper from the *Manor*, but we'll address the ladies as we move on. Trust me, we will. The earliest memories of school were not good ones. I wasn't a popular kid and I always sought attention and my grades paid for it. I failed the sixth grade and my mother made a decision that would help form my social consciousness for years to come. She placed me into Portsmouth Catholic.

Portsmouth Catholic consisted of two different schools: the elementary and the high school. It was predominately white and a whole world away from the predominately black public schools I was used to. I felt so strange and different. The bus ride was an event in itself, because the buses would pick up students from both schools. Can you imagine seven-year-olds and teenagers on the bus at the same time? Private school was expensive, and my mother made a way for me to go by taking on small jobs and cleaning the house of one of the black judges in the city, Judge Elliott. This new plan was supposed to help me academically, but what it did was magnify a low self- esteem issue that was already present. I wanted everyone to love me, so I became a class clown, pothead, athlete, artist, musician, and a Prince wanna be all this because I didn't have any identity and I was seeking some type of peace. The school was heavy into teaching religion, which was comforting to me, because of my interest in the scriptures. The school was run by Nuns. In elementary school there was a Nun named Sister Lucy. She showed the love of God and gave the fear of God at the same time. I was always in trouble. There were two older black guys who went to Catholic school. They were also from Cavalier Manor. Their names were Thomas and Slick. These two guys took me under their wings and showed me how to navigate through this new reality in my life. It was hard trying to navigate my life with my friends in the *Manor* and my life in Catholic school. I can remember going to school dressed like Prince but knowing I would not ever dare wear this in the *Manor.* So, the confusion persisted, and my grades continued to fall, but somehow, I managed to get to Portsmouth Catholic High. Something happened to me at Catholic School that I never thought would happen. I became popular, and everyone knew who I was. It was a great feeling even though I didn't know who I was. I developed a great friendship with a white boy named Vincent. We were cool and to this day I consider him one of my best friends. We both had strange upbringings and we were somewhat seen as an outcast. He would always bring big bags of weed to school then give me the rest to take home. When I got back home, I was very popular as you can imagine. In art class I was able to paint images on the desk and walls. The Art Teacher allowed me to express myself as I saw fit. Images of Prince were all over the school. I was trying to navigate my way at the tender age of 14 and it was crucial that I find a way quick, but something happened.

MINEO LA
ELLINGTON SQ

# THE GREATEST PAIN

In January of 1981, things were going accordingly. I would go to school do my routine and come home and watch Mike, Oliver's little brother. They had suffered the loss of their father a while back, and I would watch Mike until his mother would come home. I would still hang out with my regular friends when I could, but I still had to navigate the disruptions of my father and mother fighting one another. This was my life and it all became routine. There was no other way. One day when I was out playing with my friends, and as the evening approached, I had to stay over Bud and Champ's house until my parents came for me. Finally, my father came to get me without my mother which was odd, and I asked my father, "Where's mom?"

He replied, "She's still over Ms. Maurine's house."

This was a local bootlegger's house that my parents frequent. It was just outside the path of Water's Field. So, I went to sleep and as I arose for school in the morning, I noticed that my mother still was not there. So, my father instructed me to go to school while he finds out why my mom wasn't home. While at school, things were as normal, but my life as I know it was going to change for the worse. In art class I was playing and having fun creating as I love to do when a call came over the loudspeaker, "Clinton Dukes, please come to the Principal's office." The students looked at me as to say, 'what did you do this time?' This was no surprise, because it wouldn't be the first time that this announcement had been made. On my way to the office, I noticed that the journey took a little longer than usual. As I approached the office, two Nuns greeted me, one being the Principle.

She asked, "How is your mother doing?"

I said, "Fine."

We went into her office and to my surprise, my father, aunt uncle, grandmother and grandfather were all present in the room. Everyone was there except my mother; the one person who comes to every function, meeting or event that had anything to do with me. She wasn't there. They told me that my mother had died, and at that very moment, anything that was alive in me died.

I would remain dead for a very long time. Imagine a walking, dead, 15-year-old boy, with no brothers or sisters. He was left to be raised by an alcoholic father whom he hates. I didn't want to leave with them after I heard the news, so they let me stay in school to finish up the day. What happened the rest of the day in school draws a blank, but I can guarantee you one thing, that young man was numb to the core. When I arrived back to my neighborhood from school, I saw that many of my friends were there to greet me. They took that long walk with me back to my house and it is still amazing to remember young teenage boys consoling one another. One of the hardest things that I had to do and learn was how to live with the man that I hated without my mother. In my mind he took full responsibility for my mother's death. It was his fault! He killed my mother with his horrible abusive behavior, although they told me that she had a heart attack. We'll get back to that later. So, as the week went on people came by to visit and bring food, clothing, and money. People were very kind and to be honest, most of it was because of me. My Grandmother and my aunt on my mothers' side stepped in and helped with all the bills and business dealings that needed to be done. My Aunt Ruth, my mother's sister, was the one who handled all the business. In my opinion, she was the rock of the family. There were not many reasons for me to smile during the days leading up to the funeral, but I found Sanford and Son, The Three Stooges, and Spiderman very comforting. They were my only sources of laughter. On one of those days, I was able to go out with my friend, in the evening, to Waters Field where they would give me wine and weed to help me deal with the pain. This was it; this is how you deal with the pain. This is the only way to cope, and it was at this moment that I identified that you deal with pain by using. Now I had much pain, so I would need to use it often. I hated how my father would drink, and now it seems that I would follow his destructive path. The day of the funeral was a bitterly cold January day, and my mother had a great turn out. As we were about to exit the house for the funeral, I was able to look out the door and see my friend Bud standing in the street.

He walked into the house and gave me a hug. The lord knew I needed that, because I didn't have anyone. It just felt like I was all alone, but my friends were always there. I may be mistaken about this, but I believe that my mother was the first funeral in the new sanctuary at New Bethel Baptist Church. The church was cold that day. Hell, everywhere was cold. I had not seen my mother up until this point, and the pain was beginning to be unbearable. I can't remember anything about the service except when my father put his arms around me and said, "It's just you and me now baby."

I was frozen, and I didn't want this man's arm around me. This was the man who killed my mother, and I hated him. Then it happened, they open my mother's casket. When I saw her lying there, I lost it. I cried like a 4-year-old child. The pain was being released, and I couldn't control it. I lost all awareness as to where I was. When the service was over, and we exited the church to the vehicles that would transport us to the cemetery, I was still out of it. I was just there living, and existing. When we got to Roosevelt Cemetery in Chesapeake, everyone manages to make her or his way to the gravesite. I couldn't make it, I wouldn't. I stayed in the car with my head down. As a few moments went passed, I raised my head to take a look and all my friends had surrounded the car. I opened the door and let them in, and they stayed with me until the service was over. Now, I have been through a lot as you will see, but that was the most painful day that I have ever lived through, but more pain would follow.

## Aretha Dukes

PORTSMOUTH — Aretha Lee Dukes of 1507 Ellington Square, the wife of Clinton Dukes and a native of Moyock, N.C., died Sunday in her home.

She was a daughter of Moses Hall and Mahalie Askew. She was a member of New Bethel Baptist Church and its Female Usher Board 1.

Other survivors include a son, Clinton Dukes Jr. of Portsmouth; a sister, Ruth P. Shambley of Norfolk; a niece, a nephew, and aunts and uncles.

A funeral will be held at noon Saturday in New Bethel Baptist Church by the Rev. J. Marshall Whitaker. Burial will be in Roosevelt Memorial Park with Graves Funeral Home, Norfolk, in charge. The family will

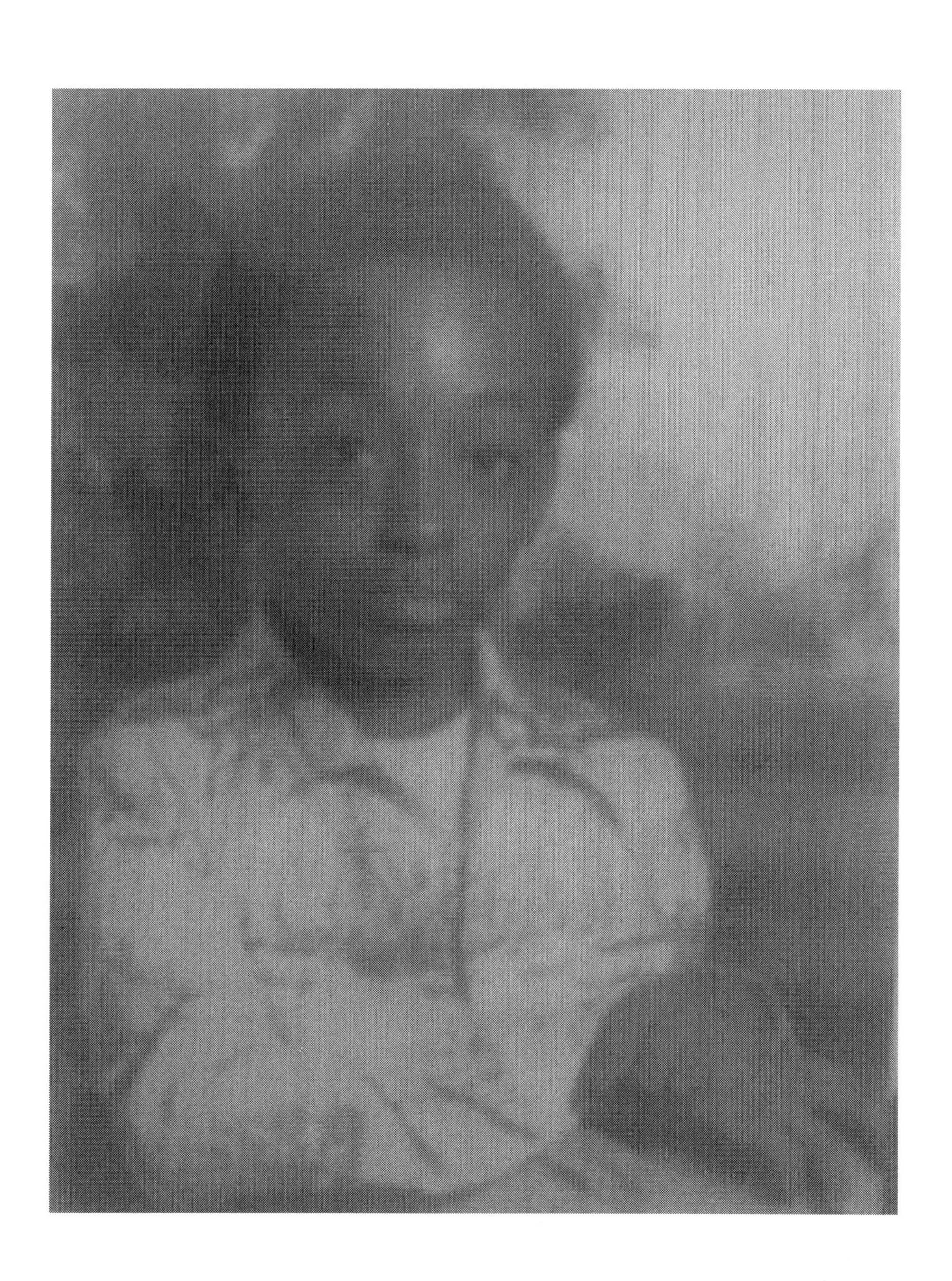

# BONNEVILLE

After the death of my mother, I remember having a meeting with my grandmother, my aunt Ruth, and my favorite cousin Linda. I loved Linda so much and she was as beautiful as she was smart. I considered her somewhere between Linda Carter and Jane Kennedy. She was maybe 6 years older than I and every time she would visit, the older guys in the neighborhood would become my instant friends. My grandmother wanted me to stay with my father because she said that I would be blessed, but I wanted to go with my cousin. She lived in DC at the time and it would be a great way to run away, but I stayed. Running away would become a part of my life later on.

So, I stayed with my father, and we managed, but my father could not keep the house anymore for reasons that I am not aware of. He was forced with a decision to make. With the counsel of my grandmother and aunt, my father decided to stay in the Cavalier Manor area, but not in another house, but in some low- income apartments called Bonneville. The decision was made because all of my friends were still here, and I was still in Catholic school. It was also told to me that the Principle at Portsmouth Catholic High School had told my grandmother that I would be able to stay at the school tuition-free, because of the love that they had for my mother. I was too young and selfish to understand the gravity of this. I hated this new environment, although it was right across the street from my church. I hated the idea that we were poor. We really were and I struggled with that. My best friend's parents had cars, houses, and nice yards. My friends had nice clothes and a few dollars in their pockets. My grandmother would drive from Norfolk to Portsmouth every other week to bring back washed clothes and cooked meals for us because we were so dysfunctional. On the first of the month she would come and take my father to the grocery store so that he could pay his monthly bills. My father's alcoholism became worse and mine was just begging. He would wake up in the middle of the day, walk into the kitchen and pee in the dishes. I was always so lost and angry. I felt trapped and needed to escape. There were a couple of black guys that I use to hang out with in Catholic school named Leon and Mike. People never knew that we use to get so drunk and high in that school. Portsmouth Catholic use to have these parties that were so wild that I would invite some of my friends from the *Manor* to attend. Those white boys really did love me. I was able to take home cases of beer and bags of weed. How did I ever survive that school? In the summer of '84, Purple Rain had come out, and Prince was in full form. At that time, I had a job inside Tower Mall at Montgomery Wards and when I wasn't doing anything I would go to the movies. I know I saw that movie at least 10 times that summer. That movie was helping to shape an identity for me. It wasn't my family, faith, or community, but Prince. See, I could dress like Prince at school. That wasn't cool to do in the *Manor*, but I could dress like Morris Day and The Time, double-breasted down. I played with some guys in a band that played all Prince Music. Vernon, Steve, and Anthony were members of the band and we even had one of our home girls, Henri, sing with us a couple of times. So that was who I was. A young teenager who thought he was Prince with no direction. I was able to hide in his rebellious, sexual, religious, political art, and I embraced every minute of it. One time, at a Catholic school dance, they asked if I my band could play. That was a pretty big deal for a group of brothers from Cavalier Manor, playing at a majority white Catholic school, and all we played was Prince. There was a white girl who hung around me while we were on stage named Lisa. Lisa was older and one of the smartest girls in the school. She was crazy about me. We walked around school holding hands kissing and sitting on each other's laps. This made people very uncomfortable. I mean who wants to see a young black, alcoholic, pothead boy, prancing around with the high school's genius princess, but that's what it was. One day Lisa met me in the back of Tower Mall, and we parked in one of the truck loading docks. We got into the back seat of the car and Lisa showed me some things. It was my first experience with oral sex, but not my last. I was turned out by this girl and I was ready to stick everything that was moving. I have had sex before, but this was on a different level. So, we continued on until school conveniently came up with a term called PDA, Public Display of Affections. This was no longer allowed. No hugging, kissing, or holding hands, and everyone knew that it was because of Lisa and I. We did have some pretty black sisters at school like Bert, Sadonna, Cynthia, Lisa, Rhonda, and Dominique. I think Cynthia and I would have gotten together if we weren't so scared of each other. They either had boyfriends, were too old, too young, or didn't want anything to do with my crazy ass. I feel like some of them felt I betrayed our race, because I was with that white girl. I was still trying to go to church, and it had its challenges, but I would try. I recall going to an evening service where there was a guest choir from a Holiness or Pentecostal church. I kept looking at this girl who was sitting in the back row and I asked her to come out to the lobby section. She was a cute girl named Lou. She stayed downtown and I really liked her, but I didn't have any other way to go see her other than with my friend Keith who had a car. I really didn't have anything for her, and her family was super strict. She had some pretty sisters too. All we did was have sex. I was starting to think that sex was the only thing I was good at, but that doesn't last long when people want more. We eventually faded away, but we kept in touch from time to time until I started my drugging.

Back at home in Bonneville, I had developed a new set of friends Icy, Robert, Robert Lee, Jeff, and Tony T. All young alcoholics, and they all loved coming to my house because my dad didn't care who came over as long as he could drink with us. I never drunk around my dad. I always went to my room even when my friends were in there drinking with my dad. I was a full-blown drunk and the only family I had was my church family which was slowly being ripped from my hands by my behavior. The church stepped in and took me up as a son. The helped me with money and other things. I played the drums every Sunday for a long time. No matter how bent I was on Saturday night I still went to church. There was a lady who lived a couple of houses down named Ms. Cotton. She was on the Usher Board that my mother was on. She made it her responsibility to become my mom, enforcer, and chaperone, and I needed it. I was sleeping with multiple girls, young, old, downtown, uptown. Quite frankly, it didn't matter. I just wanted sex and drugs. I was an accident waiting to happen. Then I fell in love.

# FIRST LOVE

So, my life up to this point was pretty reckless. I lived with an alcoholic father with no rules or boundaries at home. I was a full-blown alcoholic, sex addict, and irresponsible church boy. I was just going with the flow of whatever the day bought forth. Then, one Saturday morning out in Bonneville, Leon ad I were getting our drink on. As we were walking to the store to get some more beer, we walked through one of the cuts going through the apartments and I saw a young girl standing outside one of the doors. It was just my instinct to flirt even if I didn't like her. I just needed to validate myself like that. So, she waved back, and I ushered her to come over where we were, and she did. She looked about two years younger than I. She was pretty and had a sexy little figure. She told me that her name was Shondell and that she was over her sister's house for a birthday party. I asked her could I see her later. After all, I had more drinking to do. So, we talked on the phone all that night and I asked her to come over to my house the next day and she did. Since I had no barriers at home, I could do anything I wanted. We ended up having sex that day and the ride was on. My father didn't love many things other than alcohol, but he loved Shondell. She was too dam sweet. She was the perfect girl. She was smart, pretty and she loved the ground that I walked on. She got involved in every area of my life. She even joined the church and choir so that she could go to church with me every Sunday. She stayed over her sister's house almost every weekend just so that we could see each other. Everyone in my life loved Shon, and my homeboys did too. They saw that she was good for me and I knew it. Up unto that point, she was the best thing that ever happened to me. Even my aunt and grandmother who took over after my mom died, thought that my future wife had arrived. Hell, everyone thought that, and to tell the truth, it should have been. The one thing that Shondell was able to maneuver through was my father. She could see him cool as silk and then pissy drunk. There have been many times in the past when my father would say while drunk, "Who is in this house?"

I would tell them who it is, male or female, and he would respond, "Get the fuck out my house!"

Now his favorite response was this, "Do you know Miss Carry?"

"No Mr. Dukes!"

Then he would respond, "Well carry your ass!"

Now I'm not going to lie. That shit was funny, but my father was dead serious, but when it came to Shondell he would simply say, "Hey Shern!"

He would give her name a certain twist, hey, Shern!

It made me feel good that everyone in my life loved this girl. There was also another aspect of my life that was developing thanks to my friend Tony. He was one of the Clay Street boys I met. Tony had three brothers and a nephew, but his mother was an angel. Miss Thomas, I called her. She took me in as her child and so did the brothers. I stayed over there more than I stayed at home. It was my home away from home. This was how a home should feel. Now, I could still go over Bud, Champ and Wayne's house and still feel at home, but this place was closer, and I was entering a new chapter in my life. Tony and I were crazy as hell, trying to drink and screw everything that we saw, along with Rob, Steve, and Leon. I don't know how I made it, all the while going to Catholic school. Even though Shondell was a gift to me, I was too young, stupid, and selfish to realize it. I was still chasing girls and sex. I had everything I needed from her and we had sex like rabbits, but it was about the validation. I needed it to feel better about myself. All the while, lying and disrespecting the love that was given to me. I was all through the city chasing girls; from climbing into windows in Cavalier Manor to walking downtown to meet new girls. At Catholic school, Lisa graduated and all I did was smoke weed and get drunk. My grades were horrific, and I hadn't realized that my mother's death was a driving force behind all or most of my behaviors.

It was a shock to find out that I wasn't the only child. I learned this from a woman who said she was my cousin. She lived right behind me in Bonneville. She had two children. It was revealed to me that my father had a daughter before I was born from a woman other than my mother. I met her a couple of times and she had a son. Her son and I became close and he was almost my age. So, I had a nephew who could have easily had been my uncle, and sometimes he thought he was. My sister, it seemed to me that she had some type of mental illness issues. Sometimes I would see her, and she would just walk by, and say, "Hi Tubby," and keep going. I never knew how I felt about that, but I was glad to have a cousin in my life. She was cool and we always did things together. My sister used to come over to the house, sit down, and talk to my dad every once in a blue moon, but we never really had any conversation for each other. It wasn't because it was hard to talk to her. I really didn't know what to say to a stranger. So, just like everything else, I accepted it and continued in my existence. One day when I was coming home from one of my drinking binges or maybe it was school when I noticed that the door was cracked open. I pushed the door open slowly because I was scared to see what I might find out. I slowly walked through the house and as I was going down the hall the first room that I approached was my father's. I was hoping that he was in there sleep or passed out from a drunken spell. Well, he was in there with his pants down having sex with my sister. I didn't say a word and I went back out the door stunned and numb to what I just have seen. So, from a man who I already hated, I had to ponder what kind of monster or what kind of pain this man must be in. Even to this day, I struggle to process that. It was a part of my memory that I suppressed in my mind until now.

Back at Catholic school things were going as usual. Go to school, get high, flirt with girls, get high, and go home. I was very popular for many reasons, but it felt good to be accepted for who you wanted to be, but who was I? I was a young black, alcoholic, teenager who walked around dressed like Prince. Man, the pain that I was in. Everything I did was to try and avoid this reality. One day I went to school doing my normal routine and things changed. When my white friends and I would go to smoke weed between classes every day, we would go to the bathroom. This particular day we were getting high and one of the nuns walked in. Despite the multitude of boys in the bathroom, I was the one asked to go to the office. When I was face to face with the Principle, she was in rare form. She reminded me of how I had such a great opportunity here and how talented and smart I was. She also told me that the only reason I was still there was because she had promised my grandmother that I would have a tuition-free stay; but that opportunity has run out. They were done with Prince, and the young black boy trying to corrupt the little white girls. They were done with the drugs, laziness, irresponsibility, and fears. I was kicked out of Portsmouth Catholic High School and I was consumed with the guilt of disappointing my mother again.

# THE MANOR

Manor High School was a jewel for the youth growing up in the *Manor.* It was a fairly new school with state-of-the-art equipment. Portsmouth was known for some of its historical schools like Woodrow Wilson and I.C. Norcom, which were predominately black schools in the city, but Manor was cool and sophisticated. Most of the kids that I grew up with either went to Manor or Norcom. In 1986, I was already behind a few grades. I should have graduated in 1984, but being the attention seeker that I was, my grades paid for it. There was also one other thing that I didn't know. Public schools didn't take the credits for all the religious classes I took over the years. So, I couldn't graduate until the summer of 1987. That was a wake-up call for me. All my friends were gone, and my ass was still in school with all these young folks that I didn't even know. Wayne, one of my original homeboys, was still there. He made my transition better, but it was still hard. The Prince persona was gone, and I was all about wearing baggy pants and double-breasted suits. I didn't have much, but I did dress nice. Shondell was still in my life and we had become quite a couple. We loved each other, but it didn't stop me from pursuing other girls. In the *Manor*, there was plenty that I liked, but I felt I was too old and too broke for any of them, even though many were interested. I was determined to graduate so I studied and paid attention in class. I also realized that I was pretty smart when I put some effort into it. Even though most of my friends had graduated, we still got together and performed at talents shows that the *Manor* held every year. We won two years in a row performing as The Time. We would do Jungle Love, The Bird, and songs from the Purple Rain movie with sharp precision. We practiced so hard for those shows and we were really good. I still know the steps to both routines.

In 1987, I was able to go to the prom with Shondell. I had on a sweet tux, Miami Vice style. My friend Bud wanted me to use his car that he shared with his brother Champ. His parents didn't think it was a good idea, because of the insurance, so Bud drove Shondell and I to the prom. It was ok, but I just felt like I didn't belong. Hanging out with Icy and his girl Kim, who was Shondell's best friend, was cool.

My final year ushered around, and I was about to graduate albeit, not in the spring of 1987, but the summer of 1987, so I had to decide what I was going to do. I didn't have many options, nor did I have transportation. I didn't have a driver's license, so I decided to go into the military.

# THE MARINES

One of the easiest choices that I ever made was deciding which branch of the military I was going to join. I decided to go into the Marines, because of three basic reasons. One was the television show Gomer Pyle. The second reason was because I wanted to wear that beautiful, dress blue uniform with all my might. The third is that all my life I fought to be important. I wanted to be thought of as somebody that people would like and respect. I also tried to prove myself to people. I decided that if I went into the Marines, which was supposed to be the toughest of all military branches, that would make me look like someone. My decision was made, and I went into the Marine Corps.

So, after the summer of 1987, I graduated. I went into the United States Marine Corps Reserve in October of 1987. On the day I was leaving for boot camp I experienced something that I never saw, but one time in my life: my father cry. My grandmother, grandfather, girlfriend, and my father went with me to the bus station. Shondell was crying like a baby and my father was crying also. I haven't seen that since my mother's death, and I didn't know what to think and I didn't know what to feel. I didn't know what to experience. All I knew was that I was about to leave this toxic and painful environment. I was enroute to Paris Island, South Carolina and I didn't know what to expect. My mind was full of wonder and fear. When we got to the bus station in South Carolina they transported us to the airport where we would meet the other recruits. This was like two or three in the morning. We were all so tired when they loaded us up on the bus. Then we headed to Parris Island. They didn't want us to see how to get in for some reason and I think it was for strategic reasons or maybe even security reason but it was pitch-black and when we finally got to the island I noticed that a Drill Instructor hat stepped on the bus. He was a very polite man greeting and welcoming us to a new adventure. He told us about the pride of being a United States Marine. They told us about a little history about the island and what would be expected of us. Then three other drill instructors came on the bus and he said very politely, "Drill Instructors take over." Then all hell broke loose! They came at us yelling, screaming, cussing, and spitting in our faces. We were so tired and delusional that we didn't know what to do. We were dropping bags and falling over each other until they finally got us all lined up outside. This is where the process of becoming a United States Marine began. I was in 3rd Battalion I Company. Everybody said that 3rd Battalion was the best battalion. All the other battalions also said that about themselves. My platoon was excellent in hand-to-hand combat and marching. We won awards, but some people had real problems with the drill instructors getting in their faces. They couldn't handle it, but for me, it was quite entertaining because there was nothing that this individual could say or do to me that could match the level of pain that I had experienced with my mother's death. So, I was okay, and all I had to do was do what they told me to do, but the greatest challenge for me came when it was time to swim. I couldn't swim at all, and they would tell us to jump in the pool and swim in full gear. I struggled greatly with that, but I eventually passed to continue with my platoon. I even became a sharpshooter, I was also picked to read scriptures for the Protestant section of my platoon, I didn't think much of it because I always had a love for the scriptures and church was always in my blood. So, it was like second nature to me. So, I did it and I graduated in December of 1987, as a United States Marine. What an accomplishment, what pride, and what joy I had. I had become a Marine, one of the baddest dudes on the planet, at least that's what my mind had told me.

I graduated Boot Camp right before Christmas and I came home to such a warm welcome from friends, family, and my girlfriend. Everyone was so proud of me. I have never experienced the amount of pride that people felt towards me. Being a people-pleaser that I was, I sucked it up and took my friends out for food and drinks. I splurged on girls, but one of my proudest moments came the first Sunday that I went to church after coming home. My grandmother, aunt, grandfather, Shondell and my father were all present. This was the first time that my father had been in a church since my mother died. This made me feel good and I had my dress blues on. I didn't have anything that was awarded to me from boot camp, so I went and bought it at one of the local military shops in Norfolk. We all sat in the same row and when Reverend Whitaker was doing the announcements, he asked me to stand and Ms. Cotton, the lady who lived down the street from me, who raised me as her own child, gave him the Diploma that I received from being a Lay

Reader. When he read it out loud the whole church applauded. I was amazed at how they talked about the Christian leadership and the obligations that I had taken on as a Christian Lay Reader. It was written so well, and everyone was staring at me as I was standing. Everyone knew about my struggle. They all knew that my mother had died, and that my father was an alcoholic. So, everyone watched and listened. When he was finished, they all stood up, clapped, and cheered. My father cried sitting in his chair. I will never forget that day and it was probably the last day the Church was to feel that way about me. So, after a brief holiday stay, approximately two weeks, I went to the Twenty-nine Palms, California to become a Radio Operator. This place was destitute, and there was nothing to do. I wasn't 21 yet, so I wasn't legally able to drink, but if you stayed on the base and went to the local clubs you were able to get in just by knowing people. You could get a stamp on your hand and drink as much as you wanted. That gave me an excuse to become one of the biggest drunks ever. The military made me more of a drunk than anything else in my life. Every once in a while, we would go to Palm Springs or the San Bernardino Valley where they had a club called the Metro. The Metro had three different sections: Reggae, Rock and Roll, and New Wave or something to that effect. If you were drunk or high you could just walk through the club's different sections and think that you were on a different planet. That was the place to be and the soldiers tried to be there for every occasion. I wasn't able to have sex as much as I wanted to, because I didn't know any females there and I didn't have the money that I wanted to spend. Plus, there weren't a lot of blacks there. I did have this one white girl who was crazy about me. I didn't know what was going on about being with these white women. This one particular girl looked like the one that I was dealing with in Catholic school. We always walked and talked together. We never did anything, because, she was so afraid of the other white guys. A lot of them were very racist and very mean to her. So, I just continued to get drunk, and one day I got a call. It was my aunt Ruth who had told me that my grandmother was very ill and about to pass away. So, I asked for special permission to be able to come home early. I was in the reserves anyway, so I was able to come home and do my duty at Dam Neck in Virginia Beach. So, I said goodbye to everyone, and I came back home to Portsmouth. I came back home to Bonneville in the early part of 1988. My grandmother passed and it was a very bittersweet situation for me. In 1981, I had lost my mother and I was forced to go back to the same cemetery. As we were passing through lights traveling to the cemetery, I had no idea where my mother was buried and didn't care to know. I didn't want to look, ask, or find out.

We buried my grandmother and another level of pain was just added to the whole mountain of pain that was already on my back. It was just another level and another layer I had to deal with. I dealt with it like everything else, I'll ignore it and drink it away. So now that I am at home, I had a few bright ideas. I figured that I would go to school, get a job on the shipyard, and do my duty every once a month. It was a good idea, but I wanted to keep drinking and I wanted to keep being a people-pleaser, so I tried to do those things. I kept on drinking and smoking weed. One day while I was on duty at Virginia Beach, they gave me a drug test. When I came back the next month, I was notified that I had tested positive for marijuana. My Staff Sergeant, who was a black man, had a conversation with me. He tried to encourage me and assure me that worst case scenario is that I'll get a few office hours and lose a rank. When we went up to the Commander and he addressed me, he read off those horrible allegations in my ears. He told me that I was discharged out of the United States Marine Corps. I could hear my Staff Sergeant gasp for air as if to say that he has never seen a verdict like this before. Well once again, here I am a young black man filled with pain, guilt, and fear. Now all the peace, joy, and purpose that I had was just given back to drugs and alcohol. I was kicked out of the United States Marine Corps. How was I going to face everybody? How was I going to tell my dad? How was I going to tell my church? How was I going to tell my family? How was I going to tell my girlfriend? I was so ashamed, and I couldn't tell anyone because I didn't want anyone to think of me any less than I already felt, so I lied about it. I did get a small loan from the Credit Union at the church in which they reluctantly gave to me for good reason. I bought a used 1977 Ford LTD. It was a lemon and it was bright yellow just like a lemon. I used it to drive around. It was the first time I ever had a car and I was able to go back and forth to Virginia Beach, but when I got kicked out of the Reserves I still left as if I was going for a weekend. I would try to find a girl to stay with for the weekend, or I would spend two nights in my car with my uniform on, all to save face. The pain was just unbearable and all I knew how to do was drink and do drugs. Finally, I stopped going to Virginia Beach. I never talked about it with anyone. Most people that I knew suspected something, but they never talked about it, and for years, I never talked about it. I'm okay with it now. I didn't get a dishonorable discharge; I received a general discharge, but it was still my behavior that led to me to leave the Marine Corps. That in itself was a hard pill to swallow. Now all my lies are starting to add up on me. I didn't have a job, I wasn't in the Marines, and I didn't have any money left. I was drinking more, snorting cocaine and smoking weed. I was really in a bad way and I stopped going to church. I was playing the drums in my church for a long time and they even allowed me to take some of the drums home. In my ignorance, I allowed a guy named Paul who played the drums, use them to play at his church one Sunday, at least that's what he told me. He never returned the drums and I never had the courage to tell the people at church, because I knew that they probably wouldn't believe me. I was certain that they would believe I damaged them or sold them myself, so I stopped going to church and what little family I did have was now gone. I was totally on my own with my alcoholic father. At this time, Shondell and I were not doing too well. Something happened in our relationship that I believe to this day, destroyed it. When I was actually going to Reserve Duty prior to being kicked out of the Marines, Shondell had told me that she was going to see the doctor with her mother while I was away.

I said, “No problem. I'll see you when I get back.”

When I eventually came back that Sunday evening, I pulled up to my house and noticed that Shondell’s mother's car was parked out front. This was something that would never happen, because Shondell’s mother didn't like anything about me. She thought I was too old, too free, and too loose. She thought I didn't have any kind of future with her daughter based on the type of young man that I was. I couldn't blame her. So, as I walked into the house, I saw that everyone was sitting at the table. The amazing thing about all this was that it's around 3 or 4 in the evening and my father was totally sober. It was a complete shocker. Everyone was staring at me and my father asked me to sit down. My father was very upset and angry.

I'm looking at him asking, “What's wrong?”

I looked at Shondell and she couldn't even look me in the eye. So, her mother finally spoke and said, “Clint, Shondell and I went to the doctor's office and we found out that she was pregnant.”

So, I was like, “Okay, that's cool! We can handle that. I'm in the military and we were going to get married anyway. So, what's the problem?”

Her mother said, “We had an abortion.”

My heart dropped, and I looked at my father. For the first time I could see the anger that he had towards someone who he had felt, harmed, or wronged his son. All I could do was look at her and ask her mother, “Don't you think that I deserved to know about that? Don't you think that was the decision that Shondell and I should have made?”

Her mother just simply said, “She wasn't ready, and you weren't ready and I'm not going to allow my daughter's life to be ruined!”

So, we didn't have anything else to say to each other and from that day on, my relationship with Shondell fell apart. We tried, but too much damage had been done. We started seeing other people, but we were still sleeping with each other. It was a mess until finally, we couldn’t take it anymore and we separated.

# MICHELLE and DARRYN

1988 was one of the worst years that I ever experienced. I didn't have a job. I was living with an alcoholic father, and I was a full-blown alcoholic and addict. My girlfriend was no longer with me and my church family was all gone, but I was still hanging out with my friends. Now my friends that I grew up with when I was a young child have pretty much dissipated by now. They were still my good friends, but we didn't hang out a lot. I found my time by hanging out with guys like Icy, Robert, Jeff, Tony, Steve, Kenny, and Tony Pitt. Most of them were from Clay Street. One day we were all together driving around getting drunk. Icy and Jeff had a date with these two girls, but before they could meet up with them, we had an accident. So, when we went to the hospital and the girls met them there. Icy's girl at that time was Cheryl. She had her girlfriend with her whose name was Michelle. She was supposed to go out with Jeff. Cheryl went into the hospital, but Michelle stayed outside for some reason. We were all talking, and I made Michelle laugh-a-lot. She loved to laugh. Michelle was pretty, brown skinned, and had a nice shape. She reminded me of one of the Salt and Pepper Girls with the big earrings. She had on tight jeans and a Norfolk State jacket. I thought she was nice and sexy, but she wasn't there for me, so I just made her laugh. We just kept on drinking and finally, all the guys went home. Icy and Jeff went about their business with the ladies. A couple of days later Icy called me. He asked me if I wanted to go out with him and his girlfriend and the girl named Michelle that I met at the hospital.

I said, "Yeah that would be cool."

So, we went out. Michelle and I hit it all off pretty good. I just made her smile and laugh so much, because the Lord knows I didn't have anything else to offer her. I didn't have a lot and I wasn't the best built. I wasn't the most handsome, and I live with an alcoholic father, but I made Michelle laugh. Before you knew it, we were in a relationship. I remember one day when we were in front of Icy's house. I was standing outside, and Michelle was with me leaning against the car. Shondell came driving down Clay Street because she had family on that street. When she saw Michelle and I, she stopped the car and asked me a few questions. I told her who Michelle was and she sped off like a bat out of hell, angry and upset. I asked myself why she was angry and upset. We were not together anymore, but that's how it was. When I saw her with someone, I had feelings, and when she saw me with someone, she had feelings. That's just how it was, but I was with Michelle. We went to the movies and went out to eat. She stayed over my house from time to time. My father loved her. I believe Michelle got pregnant on Valentine's Day of 1989. Now, if I said that I wasn't happy I would be lying. If I said I wasn't scared I would be lying. What in the world was I'm going to do with a baby? I couldn't even take care of myself let alone buy a cheeseburger. I couldn't take care of anything most of the time and when we went out, Michelle gave me money or paid, because she was working, and I wasn't. All I was doing was drinking and getting high. I knew she wanted more, and some guys wanted to give her more, but I was the father of our child. So, throughout her pregnancy I tried to do what I could, but the fear and the pain in my life was just pushing me further to drink and to get high. On November 14$^{th}$, 1989, Michelle gave birth to a 9 pound. 14-ounce baby named Darryn Marcel Wright. Michelle and I had some issues with our child's name because I felt like I didn't have a say so in it. I felt like I should have been asked or been considered when naming my child. Maybe I didn't deserve to have any consideration, but this was my son. I was very proud to have a son, even though I didn't know what the hell to do.

Michelle made it clear that we we're not going to be together, but I was going to take care of my son. At least that what I told myself. I was immediately put on child support, but that system had so many flaws. It didn't do anything to help me become a man. It became a bondage situation for most of my adult life, but that's another story. I tried to come around at times and bring a few dollars, but my alcoholism was just more important than anything else. I was selfish and self-centered. I didn't visit my child as much as I should have, and I didn't give Michelle the help that she needed. So, she moved on as she should have. Now I was even more lost as the eighties were coming to an end and we were ushering in a new era and a new decade. It wouldn't be a bright one for me. It would be a decade full of confusion bondage and despair.

15

# CRACK

As I was coming home one night, I noticed there was a black Celica in the parking lot next to my apartment. I recognized the car as belonging to one of my home girls, Tonda. It was her mother's car, so I walked up to the car and tapped on the window and to my surprise it was not Tonda, but another girl. I ask her to excuse me for the interruption. I told her that I knew Tonda. She said that her name was Lisa and as we were getting acquainted, I happened to look inside of the car. This girl had a mirror on her lap full of a white powdery substance. She had alcohol swabs, a glass pipe, razor blades, and tiny bags all on her lap in the front seat. I told her she didn't have to do all this outside and that she could come to my house. I could do anything in my house as long as my dad is drunk or sleep. So, Lisa and I went into the house and she set up shop in my room. I watched in amazement how she would stir and mix up stuff; then burn it until it comes back into a hard substance. Then she would cut it and put a piece on a pipe and smoke it. I noticed that she was starting to sweat profusely, and I asked her to let me try.

She said, “Hell no! Don't you ever try this.”

I was already snorting a little bit of Coke, but I have not yet tried what she was doing. I definitely wanted some. All she wanted to do was smoke and then she would tell me to pull my pants down so she can give me head. So, this girl would come over my house every day to smoke Coke and give me head. Eventually, we started having sex every day and it wasn’t long before she passed me the pipe. When I first took a hit of crack, I didn't know what to think. I didn't feel anything out of the ordinary, but for the next five days, every time she smoked, I smoked. She said that she needed money, because she was supposed to be selling this stuff. So, I told her that I'll give her money so she would give me more to smoke. Then one morning, I woke up and there was yellow pus running out of my penis. What the Fuck!!!!! I didn't know what to do. I went to the doctor and they told me that I had Gonorrhea. I found Lisa at Cavalier Manor Field Park in a car with some guys watching a football game. I pulled over and asked could I speak to her. She got out and I shared what the doctor had told me and that it might be a good idea for her to go get checked out. She went ballistic! She went off as to think, how in the hell could I ask or tell her that she had Gonorrhea. She went on and on. I left and haven't seen her since. I was able to find out that she was running form from a lot of guys and that she was having a lot of sex with a lot of different men. I was just the one that she could come to at the end of her busy days or nights. So, Lisa and I were no more, but I had a new girlfriend. It wasn't Lisa, Shondell, or Michelle. It was crack and I had to have her at all costs. She wasn't a good girlfriend to me and once I started smoking crack I started stealing, robbing, and lying; all in that order. I didn't care about anything or anyone. The pain was just an excuse to dwell in the gutter of drugs and alcohol.

One beautiful summer morning I had the bright idea of how I could get some money. I knew that my father was going to be drunk sometime that evening. By the time my father had retired from his job at the shipyard, he had burned himself with a lit cigarette in the bed. So, every month he got a check for his retirement. My father would take that check and pay all the bills, buy groceries and that would last for the rest of the month. He would give me a few dollars for my own personal use as well. So, on this particular, first of the month, the Mailman dropped off the check and my father was sleep. This had to be around 2 p.m. and as usual my father was passed out from his early morning sprees. So, I decided that I will go cash the check for him since I was a junior and he was the senior, and we both had the same name. It was the perfect plan, so I went to the check cashing place. I was going to cash my father's check, bring all the money back and take out the normal $20 or $30 that he would give me anyway. I would put the rest in the envelope underneath this bed and go out to have a few drinks and call in the night, but that didn't happen. What actually transpired was that I cashed my father's check. I went back home and took the $20 or $30 out for myself and put the rest of his money in the envelope underneath his head below the pillow. Instead of solely drinking, I decided to buy some crack. Now if any of you know anything about crack you know that $20 isn't going to last very long. Before you knew it, I was going back and forth to my father's envelope. 2 a.m., 3 a.m., 4 a.m. and well into the wee hours of the morning until I had finally spent all of my father's monthly income. I couldn't believe what I just done. When there were no more drugs to buy and no one else was around, I was alone, full of guilt fear and shame. I didn't know what to do, so I started this pattern of running. I would run from responsibility and run from reality. I didn't have anywhere to go. I was in my early twenties and I didn't have any idea of what I was doing so I just walked the streets at night. I wasn't doing anything or going anywhere. I was just walking, existing. I couldn't go home, or I wouldn't go home. I couldn't face my father. This was my first time experiencing any type of homelessness. I wasn't homeless because I didn't have a place to go, I was homeless because I'd rather stay out in the pain and mess rather than go home and face what I had done. Well a couple of weeks went by and I finally found my way over to my nephew's house. He lived across from me in Bonneville. He let me stay over there for a couple of days. Everybody in the apartment complex new what happened, and I just sat there watching TV and drinking. I was even scared to go outside during the daytime. When we arose one morning, we heard a knock at the door. My nephew got up and went to the door. When he came back, he said, "It's your father."

I said, "Tell him that I'm not here."

He said, "Man, I'm not going to lie to your father like that, because he was my father's grandson and we're all new to this relationship."

I didn't want him to go through that and my father wasn't going away. So, I got up off the couch and walked over to the door. I saw my father standing there with his cane, older and feebler. As he watched his son approach him, I was about 20 pounds lighter, a couple of shades darker and I haven't had a shave or hair cut in weeks. I have stolen the money for food, and the rent. I took his whole check. I stole something that he had worked for his entire life and wasted it on drugs in a couple of hours, but something amazing happened that day. My father said something to me that I would never forget.

He simply looked at me and said, "Come home son, just come home."

Out of all the things that I've done, all my father had to say to me was come home. I went home that day and my father, and I never discussed it again. We never talked about it and we never said a single word about it. Now I know my father lived a certain lifestyle. I know that he was abusive, and I know he had a lot of pain, but I know now that my father loved me. I should admit that a little more than I do. That didn't stop me as I became more addicted and more abusive to drugs and alcohol. My behavior became more erratic, and I was totally out of control. I would go into stores stealing alcohol just so that my friends and I could drink. I would go into shopping centers and malls to steal electronic devices so that I could sell them, not because I wanted you to tell me how good I was at stealing. I thought that I was pretty good at it, but I couldn't have been that good judging from the numerous amounts of times that I have been arrested and incarcerated. Nevertheless, that didn't stop me. Then one day I went to jail. All of that cool stuff I had going on was gone. That Prince cool, the Morris Day cool, the smooth dressing brother with the silk tongue cool was all gone. I was a walking toothpick. I was dirty, broke, disgusting, trifling, and irresponsible and everything else you can label as such. I went from drinking beer to Mad Dog, Cisco, Wild Irish Rose, and Boone's Farm. I was becoming a bigger alcoholic than my father ever was. At least my father had a place to stay and had the ability to pay his rent and buy his own food with money that he had earned from his hard work. I didn't have shit and, I was pissed, but that didn't stop me from ripping and running. During one of my cracks sprees, I went to Tower Mall early in the morning. I had the bright idea that if I can get something electronic, I would be able to sell it so I can get my early morning fix. I actually went into Montgomery Wards, a place that I used to work when I was a teenager. I used to work in the paint department. There were still people in there that knew me, but that didn't stop me. I went to the electronic section and grabbed a large electronic keyboard off the display; not one that was in the box, but one that was on the display. I had the nerve to walk right out of the front door, right down Victory Boulevard, and right into Cavalier Manor. I walked over to a guy named Mikes house to lay low. We would drink all day until his mother came home. He would call someone to sell the merchandise I had, then get high with the money we got. This happened for weeks and weeks until I got stopped by the Police. They checked my ID and said that I matched the individual that was wanted, for shoplifting in

Tower Mall. They took me downtown questioned me and charged me with grand larceny. I was new to all of this and I tried to keep it a secret from everyone. I definitely didn't want to tell my Aunt Ruth, or anyone involved in my family. I definitely didn't want to tell my father, so I would just lie and say anything I needed to get free. I decided to take a plea agreement that would give me probation, and as a young man all I cared about was going home, Plea agreements have a way of becoming a systematic trap, especially if you are a minority or financially deprived. I received probation for the incident, 3 years with 3 years suspended. I thought I had got off scot-free, but when you're young and stupid you don't realize that when you're in the system it is a hard thing to get out of. You now have a record and if you do anything that matches your record in the future, you will probably get more time. I still haven't seen my son like I should have because, at this particular time, there is no way in the world that I wanted to go around his mother, their family or allow my son to see me in this condition. I definitely can't go now. So, I used this as my excuse to stay away. I told myself that my son doesn't need me, and he doesn't want to see me like this. Since I didn't have anything else to do, I continued to drink and get high. I continue to go into different parts of the city to steal things. When I got caught again, I would get more probation, but my good fortune would soon run out. The final straw came when I was supposed to report to my Probation Officer and I didn't go because, I knew that I have been getting high. If I went, I knew they would put me in jail, so I decided not to go. I decided to run, and I had a friend named Paul who graduated with me from Manor High School. He became a Sheriff's Deputy. He used to drive through the neighborhoods a lot and we would see each other and chat. On this one particular day, he came looking for me. He came to my house and my son and Michelle were there. My father knew Paul and he came in the house and chatted with my dad for a few. I went and hid in the closet. Paul came looking for me and tapped on the closet door.

He said, "Hey man, I need to talk to you."

I talked to him and I asked him not to let my son see me in handcuffs. Paul went outside and walked with me. He let me sit in the front of the car and I told them that I would be back, and we drove off. Paul stopped the car around the block to put the handcuffs on me.

He took me to jail, but my father bonded me out, only to have me catch another charge while I was on bail for going into a 7' Eleven on Airline and Greenwood to steal a bottle of Cisco. This took place in less than three days. So, when I finally did go to Court the Judge finally gave me 3 years. I stayed in the Portsmouth City Jail until it was time for me the go to prison.

# PRISON

When I was shipped to prison it was one of the most eye-opening experiences that I can remember. I remember being shackled, hands and feet, leaving Portsmouth City Jail. Inmates were being transported to different locations in a tiny and cramped van. My destination was the Buckingham Correctional Unit. As we approached, I saw a huge fence with gun towers. The massive size of the institution itself was so intimidating that I didn't know what to expect. All I really knew about prison was what inmates told me in the jail and what I've seen in the movies. I was afraid of getting into fights. I heard about the rapes, killings and all those other things that were in our social consciousness that we talked about, but all I could do was focus on that song that Ice-T wrote called the Gun Tower. As I approached and got closer my nerves flew. When we got into the institution, we all got locked up. We were stripped buck-naked and sprayed down with a solution of vinegar and water. We were treated like cattle moving through a line. One of the scariest things that one could experience is walking into your living quarters, pod or whatever they might want to call it. Now being the new guy, I didn't know anyone, and I was all by myself. I was afraid, angry, and lonely. I didn't know what to think or how I would survive. How did I allow myself to get to this point in my life? I don't remember exactly how old I was, but I couldn't have been no more than 25 at the time. I was a young, bright, 25-year-old black man whose life was thrown away because of drugs, and alcohol. Also, he didn't know how to face his pain and didn't care to face it. It was a hard task trying to navigate my way to learn who was who, where to go, where not to go, who to talk to, and who not to talk to. So, the most easiest and comfortable thing to do was to go around people who went to church. I was comfortable and familiar with church, although I wasn't the best Christian in the world. The Lord knows I was far from a spiritual person, but I had a lot of religious knowledge in my head. They had a nice choir at Buckingham, and I would sit outside while the guys were working out and listen to them sing. The guys always wanted me to come and join, but I never did. I would just go workout, sit, and listen. So, one day this gentleman gave me a Bible and a commentary. When I got back to my cell that day, the next morning, something had happened on the yard. The prison was on lockdown for a whole month. So, I started to do something that I never did before. I opened the Bible and started reading and I read, and I read, and I read. I grabbed the commentary and I looked up the scriptures. I looked to see what the commentary was saying, and I applied it. Something was very strange was going on with me. I had the ability to remember certain things that I read, and I had a unique way to explain it in my head. I was in my cell with one of the gentlemen. He was very quiet, so all I did was read and ponder to myself. At the end of the lockdown I went out and I met with the gentleman from the choir. I told him that I really appreciated the gift that he gave me, and he said, "Thank you!"

I told him that when I get out, I would really like to be able to contact him, because I was there just for receiving. I would only be there for a couple of months until they send me to another facility where I would spend my remaining time. The brother just looked at me and said, "Brother, God bless you! I love you and don't worry about giving me your address man, I got three life sentences. I'm not going anywhere. I will be here until I die."

That struck me and it hit me hard, because here was this gentleman who was kind, considerate and one of the nicest people I ever met. This gentleman will never get out of prison. I didn't know how to process that, so I just shook his hand and told him thank you. About three weeks later I was shipped to my next facility. This is a work facility called Camp 9 in Rustburg, Virginia. There was nothing, but rednecks and Jerry Falwell Bible toters, because Rustburg was right next to Liberty University in Lynchburg.

Camp 9 was an old run-down facility. A sixties slave like mentality was felt all over the prison, but it was good fellowship amongst the brothers there. I would go out with one of the road crews throughout the City of Rustburg and cut shrubs and weeds. It was a very mundane job. I would come back to the facility, and workout, but I also continued to study, and I found comfort in going to church. There was a white guy there who was the leader of the Christian fellowship there.

He would always set up the services and greet the volunteers who came in. He kept us informed and tried to be a good leader. I would often go to Bible study eager to learn and eager to share. The people were always responsive to me. Something was going on with me. I spoke with authority, and I was able to remember stuff that I wrote. I was able to apply it to everyday situations. For some reason I was good at that and people would listen. Donnie became frustrated and irritated, but he never shared why. He wanted to give up the fellowship, so he turned the duties of the fellowship over to me. He even gave me his Bible. It was a very expensive study Bible and he said he just wanted to give it to me and that he was done. I tried to ask him why, but he would never answer. It disturbed me very deeply that he did this, and I felt guilty, because he may have been doing this because of me. He didn't change his mind and he stopped coming to church, so I took over the duties. I became the worship leader for the facility, and I was good at it. When the volunteers came in, I would teach, and I would preach. I was able to set up special programs for Christmas and Thanksgiving and I even became a leader in the facility. I had respect among the staff and the inmates and that made me feel good. It gave me a sense of respect that I never really had in my life. Everybody around me, regardless of their occupation or position in life, looked to me for leadership or example. That is still one of the biggest drugs that I have ever had. The drug of acceptance is a hard drug to overcome. One day, on one of the worksite details, we were sharpening axes. We were joking with each other and I made a mistake. I slipped and cut my hand. I split my hand wide open and we quickly loaded the van up to go back to the facility and then I was sent to the hospital in Lynchburg. To this day I used this situation as a teaching tool about how great pain unmanaged can cause us not to function in the manner that we were created to function. At this particular time, my hand couldn't function, but that's another book. I received some stitches and was sent back to the facility. They no longer allowed me to go out to the Work Camp. They sent me to the heavy equipment school that they had on the facility. We went out to large land areas around the facility that had bulldozers, backhoes, tractors, and things of that nature.

We were taught how to use them, but to be honest, I wasn't very good at it. After nine months I was called to go to another facility. I had put in for a program called Capital Construction. It was supposed to be a step closer to going home. So, they sent me to north housing unit where I would stay and go to different facilities to work. I was a part of a group that went out to Camp 29 in Honaker, Virginia. It is located near the southwestern part of Virginia near the Tennessee border. The trip there was terrifying. We rolled around mountaintops, circling the edges handcuffed and shackled. If one of those buses would have slipped and rolled down those mountains, we were dead, but we made it to Camp 29. The Capital Construction Crew was tasked with fixing the metal roofs on the buildings. It was a good job and I learned a lot. We got paid a little more than everybody else. Most people got paid .29 to .35 cents for their jobs on the facility. Capital Construction got paid maybe $1.25 or something to that degree. So, we were big shots in everybody's eyes. Once again, I became a Worship Leader there and had the opportunity to fellowship with all religions. I talked to Jehovah's Witnesses, Muslims and everybody who came into the facility to share. I wanted to be a part of it so I can learn from them, understand what they believe, and share my viewpoints. This made me a well-rounded teacher, because of my abilities to listen and respect someone else's beliefs. It seems like I was able to function in this environment. Everything was going smooth. I didn't have any issues with anyone. Most people had respect for me, even if they didn't agree with my religious philosophies. Everybody respected me, because I showed love for everyone. I learned a great deal about perceptions, and stereotypes being in the mountains. You see that most people just want to live and be able to take care of their families, but just like most people, they have their prejudices too. I was doing pretty well in prison and a lot of it had to do with God's grace that was a put on my life, but I was in an organized environment. I grew up in so much chaos that this structured environment was something that I could flourish in. Since I didn't have any issues or any institutional history that was negative, I put in for work release and I got it. So, in the beginning of 1994, I made work release and I left the mountains of Honaker, Virginia and I was transported to the Southampton County Work Release Facility. This was a pretty big deal and it meant that I was close to going home. I was also going home with some money in my pocket. It was a small facility right next to the Southampton Prison which was a huge facility full of bad dudes with bad attitudes. There were always fights, lockdowns and killings in the facility, but I was next door to it. I loved the facility I was in because of the administration and the other was for its peace. It was like heaven; it was peaceful and most of the guys either went to work, came from work or getting ready to go home. It was a place that no one stayed any more than six months. The best job there was the peanut factory, but most of the guys wanted to go to Perdue because of the number of women that were there. I went to Perdue. The Perdue Chicken Plant was in Emporia, Virginia on Route 58. It was very large facility. I believe about 600 to 800 people worked there on different shifts. I was fortunate enough to get into the quality assurance position. The guy who had that job from the camp went home and I was next in line to get that job. The first day I went in all the guys who we're also at the facility told me to go into the break room to wait for the Supervisor to come and talk to me. When I went into the break room it was like walking into an arena. There were people everywhere. I wasn't quite ready for what I was about to see. I haven't been around so many people in so long and all the women were looking at me. Now, I never claimed to be the best-looking guy and I told you how I felt about myself as a child, but by this time I had been incarcerated so long and I exercised on a regular basis. I was looking pretty good and those women knew that I was in prison. So, I was already a target. It was a very smooth job. All I was responsible for doing was checking weights and counting certain amounts of chicken in totes. When most other people were standing in the line cutting chicken all day long, I had opportunity to walk around and check out my surroundings. At the end of every shift I was able to leave early about 30 minutes so that I can put the report into the computer and the next shift would always be getting ready to come in. There were always these two girls who were present to hand out certain tools and gloves to the people coming in for the next shift. I always looked at this one girl named Terry. Terry was about six foot, maybe six foot one. She was dark, beautiful, angelic, and special. One day I just walked up to her and introduced myself and she reached out her hand to shake mine.

She said, “Hello my name is Terry.”

Terry and I exchanged numbers. I was honest with her and told her where I was, as if she didn't already know. We became a couple. Everybody thought we were the perfect couple and I thought that I was going to marry her, but there was a problem. There were other women trying to get my attention, but no other girl got my attention more than a girl named Hattie. She worked in the supply room. During the day shift I would always go up to get my gloves and whatever else that I needed, and she would always look at me with those beautiful eyes. She was slim, older, and very pretty. I had a lot of attention from the women and it was so confusing to me, because of the way that I grew up. I didn't get any attention from the girls growing up, and now I was getting plenty. So, I spent my time in the day with Hattie, but everyone knew that I was in a relationship with Terry. Hattie was smooth, elegant, and sexy. Terry was kind, built and gorgeous. I was really confused for a long time as to who my heart really belonged to. One week, when Hattie was on vacation. It so happened to be the same week of Terry's birthday. I wanted to do something very nice and sweet, so I decided to buy her a ring. I gave it to her in the back of the building at a very quiet moment. When the people found out they went crazy. I was just giving it to her as a birthday present, but everybody thought it was an engagement ring. Deep inside I thought it could have been, but I didn't want it to be done here in that way. I didn't have any choice. I had to give it to her. She loved it and she was crying. She was happy and we really loved each other, we really did. We were going to get married eventually after I got out. At least that was the plan. The next week when Hattie got back from vacation, her girlfriend had told her that I gave Terry a ring and she lost her mind. She was hollering and screaming all through the plant, "I can't believe you did that! Why would you do that? What about us?"

So, I went through that brutal week and Hattie didn't speak to me for a long time, but Terry and I were still good until she found out about Hattie. It turned out that those two had history. It seems that Terry had a boyfriend in the past whom Hattie was involved with in some way, so this is very discouraging for Terry. I made a promise to her that it was all about her, and it was all about her. Nevertheless, I was still flirting with other girls and asking other girls to come see me when I got out in Portsmouth, but it was all about Terry in some type of selfish, foolish way. I just couldn't seem to get rid of that selfish desire to validate myself with other women. During this three-year period, I had become a spiritual man, a religious man, a leader, a spokesman, and an example to a lot of men and a lot of the people who were in this plant. They looked up to me and respected me, regardless of my selfishness and self-centeredness. I still spoke of God often and talked about the power of His will in my life, but I was still functioning as a little boy trying to get attention from every little girl. So, when my time was finally up, I was ready to go home, and Terry came to pick me up in a rental car. She was looking beautiful, like a tall, dark skinned Sade and I knew that she was going to be mine that night. I had about $1,500 at my disposal, but I was going back to Portsmouth. I was going back to live with my father. I was scared to death and I didn't know what to expect. At this time, my father had now moved to Academy Park. It was an old naval housing section of the city that was run down. I was no longer in the *Manor,* and it was a step down from Bonneville Apartments. It just went from bad to worse, so Terry and I made the trip from Southampton County to Portsmouth, Virginia.

# COMING HOME

When we drove to Portsmouth, I just wanted to drive around. I didn't want anyone to know I was home yet. I just wanted to drive around and see my beautiful home that I always loved. I still do, but at this particular time, I didn't want to go to Academy Park. I didn't want to go into the junk and the filth of my father's house, and I didn't want to be reminded that I would be coming home to this mess again. So, Terry and I got a room downtown and spent an incredible night together. I have waited for this moment for so long and we finally had a beautiful night. Everything was perfect except for the fact that I knew that I had to go home. The next morning, I went to my father's house and I saw how dirty and unmanaged the place had been and it was very disturbing. I was kind of embarrassed to allow Terry to see it, but I'd already told her about my upbringing and the kind of atmosphere that she might expect to see. She just stepped right in without any hesitation. I looked her in the eyes and told her goodbye and I started my life over again. An ex-convict coming out of prison with a world of potential and promise.

For the first time, my father and I talked and drank beer together. I gave him money and things seemed to go well for a while. A lot of my friends came over to see me throughout the next few weeks. I would spend money on beer and go see the old people from Cavalier Manor. We would go to certain parties and a lot of people were glad to see me. It was good to be seen. My first love, Shondell, made it her business to come see me no matter who she was with. We were no longer together, but we still continued to have sex. We really didn't break up. We were pulled part, because of the abortion situation. My son, Darryn, was almost 5 years old. Michelle would bring him over to see me. Michelle and I would try to connect every once in a while. I would try to get with her sexually on multiple occasions, but she was done. Maybe a touch, but that's as far as she wanted to go. I think I caused too much damage with her. I guess she vowed to never have sex with me again. Regardless of whatever I did in my life, and no matter how bad I was, she never denied me the right to see my son and I'm grateful to her for that. Even though I wasn't working at Perdue anymore, Perdue wasn't done with me.

There were four or five women that wanted to come see me when I got released and they all came one week after another. They came from Emporia, Franklin, Yale, and Stony Point. They were coming every week to spend the night with me, just one night. I don't know what was going on, but they were coming. Terry was my girl and I loved that woman. I wish I could have married her, but I wasn't financially stable or ready to marry her. Terry would come every week. She would spend the weekend here or she would take me back to Emporia to spend the weekend with her. We did this almost every weekend for about 2 months while I was trying to organize the house and get my room together that I was staying in. I found a box full of old paperwork and I looked in it. I saw my mother's death certificate. I looked at it and I read it.

I asked my father, “How did you say my mother died?”

My father said, “She died from a heart attack.”

I said, “I have her death certificate right here and it says that she died from acute alcohol poison.”

My father got very quiet. He said, “What does that mean?”

I didn't know what it meant myself, but after doing some research, and asking him a few questions, it basically boiled down to this. My mother drunk herself to death. That was a hard pill for me to swallow. My mother was in so much pain trying to be a church woman, keep up with the Joneses, raise a child, put up with an alcoholic husband with low income, and put me through Catholic school. The misery and pressure were too much. My mother had to find peace with alcohol, but on that one particular night, she needed more comfort than her body could handle. So, with that new information I just tried to get used to being home after all these years. It's good to have my son back and it's good to have my friends around as well, but I started to drink again when I came home. I thought I could handle it. I thought I would be okay, but this is the constant lie and deception I told myself. As long as I don’t get high, I’ll be ok. Trying to be a player and trying to be slick only magnified my alcohol use.

One day I was walking to the Town Mall to cash a check that the prison had sent me. My money was already running low and I had already started smoking crack a little bit, but not noticeably. At least that's what I thought. I went through the drive-thru, but I didn't have a car, so I stood in the line when this woman in the car behind me honked the horn. She wanted me to get in her car so I could wait in line with her. So, I got in the car and we talked and flirted. I cashed my check and told her thanks, but she wanted to take me home. I said no, because I was still ashamed of where I lived. I have been ashamed of where I live since moving from Bonneville. After I got out the car, I told her I'll jog home. I was still in excellent shape and I was still looking good, but my spiritual and mental state wasn't good. She gave me her phone number and a couple days later I called her. She invited me over to her house and we smoked crack all night long. I couldn't have sex because I couldn't get an erection while smoking crack. It wasn't long before I had spent all my money. In the morning I went home broke again. So now, all my money is gone from the prison, and I still didn't have a job. I'm an alcoholic, my crack addiction is back, and I'm living at home with my alcoholic father. So, all I knew how to do was walk around, drink and get high. I still managed to have a few girls that would come and see me from Emporia, but that would soon end. Terry was already coming every weekend to pick me up. Either she would stay in Portsmouth or we would drive back to Emporia. On this particular weekend she came to stay in Portsmouth, and I had already been smoking crack for a couple of weeks and I lost a little weight. If she noticed she didn't say anything, but I felt it. My clothes didn't fit like they used to, and my waves weren't kicking like they used to. My skin was a little darker and I'm not acting right. Nevertheless, Terry never said anything because she loved me or maybe she just didn't recognize it. So, we left to go get a hotel room so that we could spend the night together. We went and got something to eat and I made up a lie that some guys have been looking for my father while I was incarcerated. They found out where I was at and I had to pay them $25 because I didn't want them to hurt my father.

So Terry went to the ATM machine and gave me $25. I left her in the hotel room and took her car to buy some crack. I smoked the crack and came back to the room and asked for more money. I went and smoked crack, came back to the room and asked for more money. All the while, using the same excuse, but this last time, I tried to be a little slicker and sweeter.

I said, "Baby I promise this is it and when I come back to the room I want you to come to the door with no clothes on, butt naked, and we going to do the dam thing!"

So, she got back into her car and went to the ATM machine. She game gave me some more money and I went and smoked crack. By the time I came back to the room it was around 3 a.m. She opened the door all elegant and built like a brick house waiting for me to come in and take her. I wanted to take her, but the crack was stronger. I went in the room sat down told her that I need some more money. She just looked at me with disgust on her face, put her clothes on and went out to the ATM machine again gave me some money. I went out and did the same exact thing and when I finally came back to the room it was around 9 or 10 a.m. It was getting close to check out time. Terry was so angry, and she wouldn't speak one single word to me. I knew she was mad, and I felt so bad and ashamed, but I was hooked, and I was bad off. I had only been out of prison maybe two months. As we drove to my house that morning it was silent. I had to make up another lie or tell her something so that I could get some more money, because I wasn't done smoking crack yet. Even though the night was over, and the day was just beginning. So, I made up another tale that I was trying to obtain a job and I needed some tools. I asked her to loan me $75 until I could pay her back. She just looked at me and went to the ATM machine and got $75 out and threw it in my lap.

She took the receipt and looked at it and she said, "See this Duke? I spent $400 in one night and I didn't even get a wet ass."

Terry let me out the car. I never felt so bad or ashamed in my life as I did that day, but more shame was to come. Later that week, I was on one of my walking sprees throughout the city. I didn't have money so I would steal wine from different stores on my journey from Academy Park to downtown. I also went into stores to steal items for crack money, but my time again, was short lived. I got arrested again and this time I didn't get a bond. I thought I would call Terry to let her know what was going on, so I called collect. I couldn't get an answer and I called over and over. Eventually I got contact with her thru her little sister. The sister who loved me, and thought I was the greatest guy ever. That little girl was so proud of me and showed me so much love when I first met them. She told me on the phone that my sister doesn't want to talk to you anymore Duke, and please don't call us anymore, and hung up the phone. I knew that I had messed up one of the best things that I had in my life. Terry was such an awesome woman. She was so kind, and sweet. She loved me with everything that she had unconditionally, and I messed that up. It was something else that I lost over drugs and alcohol. When would it end? When would it be over? Once again, I find myself in a jail cell waiting to go to prison, because of drugs and alcohol. Why couldn't I stop? How come I could be in jail and be an outstanding citizen, preach and teach what guys needed and become a great example in that organized environment, get out and almost immediately turn to drugs and alcohol? I have become a trifling, irresponsible, worthless, cheater, liar, and thief, all within the turn of a key. Everyone was pretty much done with me. All my family, and friends, even the ones who were petty and were only around me just to drink or get high. No one wanted to have anything to do with me. My father was the only one still sending me a few dollars, but he didn't have it to give. If he chose not to, I would have understood, because his son kept going to jail and prison. What was wrong with me? Why I couldn't stop this time? Prison was a little more painful for me, because I was older, and everybody seemed to be a little bit younger. I went to a place called James River Work Center, and once again, I became a leader and example to the community. I became one of the Christian worship leaders at that place. I taught, and preached even though I felt unworthy, but something kept urging me. You got something to say, say it. You got something to preach, preach it. Use your gifts and you will be ok. So, this is what I did in prison. I worked out, played chess, read the Bible and I was a preacher. Yes, I was a jail house preacher. I was given a job at the James River Book Center on one of the road gangs that went to the Goochland Women's Prison.

The women's prison in Goochland was huge and looked like a college campus. I was on one of the work crews that went around and did different odd jobs and maintained the grounds. Everywhere we went women would try to talk to us. They would throw phone numbers and even throw panties at us. I got three different addresses every week. Having a girl to write or somebody who was interested in you made you feel good. Some of those girls had life sentences and were going to die in prison. They didn't really care about anything and at any given moment you walked past one of their housing units you can see one of the girls licking each other or flashing us. All the guys on my crew got phone numbers all the time, but I might have been the worst. I had girls sending me letters, sometime four or five a day. My life even got threatened by one of them when they found out that I was writing another one, but something changed my attitude about that real quick on the prison grounds. There was this real big house that looks like a plantation house, and it had bobbed wire around it. This was for the real violent women. We were allowed to go in and cut the grass, paint or whatever else they might need us to do. One of the guys had a girl there that he was writing. Every time that we will go, she would always tell him to come to the fence or the screen doors so that she could flash him and show him some stuff. On this one particular day, she asked him to come to the screen door.

She was talking all sexy to him and then said, "Wait here baby!" Then she went to the back.

Now we all were kind of standing around looking, because we wanted to see what she was flashing. My crew mate was proud to have a woman that would flash everybody, and we were proud to look. When she came back to the screen door, she had a cup full of hot microwaved piss and threw it on him. She told him that he better not ever talk to another one of these bitches here on this facility. I can still see his reaction and I can still smell the combination of urine and burning flesh. The officer with us hurried up and loaded us into the van. I would never forget that day and I never wrote any woman from that prison again, but something else was going on during that time also. This occurred during the OJ trial and everybody was anticipating the verdict to come down. It was like a rich verses poor thing or a white verses black thing.

The racial overtones were incredible, especially for those of us in prison. Now OJ never really cared about many of us in the black community, but for some reason, we wanted him to get off; even though many of us believe that he did it. We were cutting grass on the lawn and we heard a big uproar; a huge cheer a sound that you would never hear in a prison. It was a sound of jubilance, hope and gratitude. The girls had just heard that OJ was found not guilty. It seemed that many black people were proud and happy, and a lot of white people weren't. Even to this day I believe that OJ might have done it, but it felt good to see that someone escaped this hostile system that has wronged so many of us. One wrong doesn't make a right, but hey it is what it is. So, after some good behavior I was able to make work release again. I was released from the James River Work Center and was transported to the Men's Work Release Facility in Chesterfield, Virginia. Once again, I have been blessed in my journey and I have received favor. I was able to go to a facility where I can once again come home with enough money to help myself, get situated and try a new beginning. The work release facility was a place just outside of Richmond. As you know, I immediately became in leadership at the church. I was able to function so well in a controlled environment. I was such a good individual trying to function in an organized environment, and everything I touched turned to gold. People thought I was the greatest thing ever, but deep down inside I still had demons that had not dealt with. I was still selfish, self-centered, and I was still full of fear. I was still the little 13-year-old kid that had lost his mother, but I was able to manage. I ended up getting a job at one of the car washes in Richmond. I immediately excelled and became one of the supervisors. It seemed that every time that I was off drugs and alcohol, great things always came to me. Not only with job opportunities, but also with the ladies. I don't know if it was because of my personality, spirituality, looks or whatever, but I still saw myself as the skinny, little, alcoholic, motherless boy. I tended to attract a lot of women there. Men in prison just looked different; our skin, builds and our attitudes. Women were used to dealing with men on the street who were always high, or drunk. Women were coming to the car wash to see me and bring me food.

Some of them even came to visit me at the prison. I really didn't know any of these women. I was still missing Terry and I was still hurt, because I hadn't talked to her or asked for her forgiveness. I was still holding on to the fact that maybe I can find her one day, but that day never came. So, I just kept entertaining myself with the hope of meeting somebody who could fill that void.

# MARRIAGE

One day I saw this lady who lived behind the car wash and she walked past me. I approached her and asked her name and I told her mine. She worked at a Kmart down the street on Midlothian Turnpike. We communicated and exchanged information. She had one grown son and she was 15 years older than I. The age difference didn't bother me, and it didn't bother her. I appeared to be a highly religious person and so did she. She wanted to be married and I wanted to be married. There were so many things that I didn't share and there were so many things that she didn't share with me, but we believed that we loved each other. I thought that we loved each other and everybody who was at the carwash believed that I had a great thing. I always had the opportunity and the blessing to have these beautiful and great women in my life. Here is another one that I'm willing to marry. To be honest, there was another lady who I really liked; she was from Norfolk. She lived in Richmond and she was a devout Christian. She was fine and she really did like me, but I really wanted to be with the first lady. She would make me plates and come visit me. She would make food for the other guys and she was really a nice woman. I knew that she had been through some things, because of what she had told me. I shared a few things with her also. It all seemed like a perfect fit, and we were to be married. I still wasn't quite sure what to do, because I was still liking the young lady from Norfolk. My future wife had a son who was about to go into the military, and it was her only son. The day he left she walked over to the car wash with her eyes full of tears, and runny nose. She looked like she had just been through hell. I asked her what was wrong, and she told me that her son was gone, and the pain on her face was terrible. She said that she was going to be all alone, and it was then that something had hit me.

I said, "No you're not, because we are going to be married."

That day I decided that it was going to be her. It was hard to let Ms. Norfolk go, but I felt God was leading me in this direction. So, the day upon my release, we went down to the courthouse and got married. I remember, there was a male friend of hers named Reverend Mason, I believe. He was asking me a question, and I remember stalling. I can't recall which question that was asked, but I was quiet. I looked at him and then I looked at her and she said, “Proceed!”

I didn't say a word. I just sat there and watched, because I wanted to do the right thing, but I just didn't know if I was doing the right thing. Nevertheless, I did. So, on November 12, 1996, the very same day that I was released from prison, I got married to a woman I knew less than 6 months.

I moved in with her and she lived in one of the projects in Richmond called Jefferson Village. It had a reputation, but I didn't know much about Richmond anyway. I wasn’t worried, because I was from Portsmouth. I lived in Bonneville, and Academy Park. I have also been in and out of prison, so it didn't seem that bad to me. My honeymoon was spent in her apartment that night. We got some champagne from Food Lion, watched Toy Story, and made love. We were both nervous and uncomfortable, but we learned how to settle in, but a demon followed me into my marriage. Occasionally, on rainy days when I didn't have to work, I would just stay home. Every once in a while, I would look across the parking lot of the projects and see certain activities taking place. I saw guys and girls walking to one particular apartment and coming out very quickly. There was a light skin girl and dark skin girl that lived there. Me, being the crackhead that I was always recognized those activities. So, I would go out to the trash can when I really didn't need to, look over there and nod my head like what's up. The dark-skinned girl always gave me a little more attention than I should have had. She would nod her head back so I would say, “What's up?”

Then she would say, “What's up?”

So, I walked over there and found out that they were selling crack. Wow, what a revelation! Who would have possibly known that? Yeah right. So, after my terrible history with drugs and alcohol, I decided to buy some crack. Now, I came home with a few thousand dollars in my pocket. I was in pretty good shape, but nevertheless, I spent that first $20. I walked to the store, got me a can of soda and a pack of cigarettes. I didn't even smoke cigarettes, but I got them just so I can get some ashes to put on my can. I have only been home a couple of weeks as newlyweds, but I was about to go smoke some crack.

I haven't had anything in a couple of years. On top of that I was in a strange place and environment. I smoked the crack in the bathroom and this feeling of euphoria rolled up in me and it was all she wrote. All the praying, all the scriptures, all the teaching, and all the preaching got lit up in smoke. I kept going back and forth on a continuous basis. I was able to get away with it for a couple of days, then money started getting low, and I started to miss days from work. Then I would get crack on credit. They all knew that I worked at the carwash, so it wouldn't be any problem. Plus, the girl kind of liked me, so I thought. She could have just been using her seductive ways to get my dumb ass to spend more money. Sometimes she would meet me in between the doors of the apartment complexes. We would just stand there waiting for somebody to make a move. She was daring me to touch her or kiss her, but I kept freezing up for some reason. I couldn't do it and I knew she wanted me to, but as time went on my appeal started to disappear. I was no longer the built guy that came out of prison and I was no longer the right complexioned gentleman that I appeared to be. I had lost a lot of weight and I looked just like a regular crackhead on the street. I finally lost my job, and I eventually got another job at the Goodwill across the street. It was a nice atmosphere and I was doing janitorial work. I thought that change of pace would help me, but every time I got paid, I snuck around to certain houses in the projects to get high. Eventually I started staying out later; much later than I wanted to. I would get into more arguments with her and one day the shit would hit the fan.

One particular day when I didn't have any money, I decided to go into my stepson's room and sell some of the game systems that he had. How in the world could I steal from a young man that I didn't even know and whose mother I said I loved? I had met him a few times while I was at the car wash, but by the time we got married, he had already left and went to the Army. I was supposed to take care of his mother. I've only been married a few months and I'm totally cracked out. I didn't have any of the money that I brought home from prison and I can't save any work money, because I smoke it all up. Any money I gave to my wife I asked for back later, and now I am going into his room to steal some of his items. Items that his mother probably bought with her hard-earned money or he bought with his hard-earned money. All this to buy some drugs that will last me only a few seconds. What selfishness. What total disregard and disrespect for someone that you say that you love. Nevertheless, it does not matter, because to me, getting high is the only thing that matters. It's about what you want, how you want it and when you want it. You are driven by selfishness and self-centeredness that is unmatched by anything that you hold dear. So, after being out all night for the first time in this new marriage, I came home to a locked door. My wife wasn't going to allow me to come in and she was furious. I sat on the steps waiting for her to come in. When she finally arrived, she was with her sister and her boyfriend. They just looked at me with despair and disgust. I will never forget the looks on their faces when they saw me for the first time, sitting on the porch, after being out for days. The marriage wasn't over, but we kept trying. My wife wasn't able to understand the magnitude of the drug addiction that I had, and I was starting to realize the magnitude of jealousy that she had. Now, I have to admit that hanging out all times of night getting high with strange women would make someone jealous, but this was different. We'll take a look at some of this later. I fell into a vicious cycle, while living on the South-Side of Richmond. I couldn't find a job so I would often go to day labor sites, make some money, go get a beer or two, and the next thing you know, I have smoked it up with no money left, then I would come home. Sometimes I just couldn't come home. I just couldn't stop and then when I felt like I wanted to stop, it was too late. Sometimes I would be gone two or three times a week. I would come home when I got tired. When I came home the arguments started. I'd be okay for a week or two, then I'd go out and drink again. What is the problem? What's wrong with you? You've got too much talent, and you've got too much going on. You're too gifted to be allowing yourself to be in this situation. It seems that I would just keep going and going and all of this started once I took a drink. I knew the craving would start once I took a drink, but it didn't do any good. Alcohol was my friend. Alcohol kept me warm. Alcohol kept me company and it made me courageous. Alcohol was everything to me. I had two masters; one was God while I was in prison, and the other one was alcohol when I was out of prison? How come I was not able to serve God when I'm free?

How come I can't be that leader in my community? How come I don't want to give up the most destructive thing in my life that causes so much pain to others? I grew up in church and I knew about God, but I was not allowing God to rule in my life. So finally, it happened. I got locked up again for stealing. I was hanging with a couple of guys and we decided to go into a mall. We would go in and take clothing, tools or whatever we could get our hands on all so we can sell to get high. Richmond City Jail was no joke. Now I had been to Portsmouth jail and I thought it was pretty bad, because it was tight and cramped, but Richmond jail was huge, and it was overcrowded. It didn't have any air conditioning and there were fights all the time. Again, this place was no joke, but just like any other institutional setting, I knew what I had to do. Once I got in, I'd start working out, play chess and I'd start teaching bible classes. That's exactly what I did, but it took me a few weeks to start teaching. Even in jail you can't just come in off the street all cracked up and start preaching. Wherever I went after being locked up, I become a leader and received great respect from people. So why couldn't I have the respect on the streets? I would do a month, 3 months or a year, multiple times, get out and repeat the same thing. When was it going to end? Why was this lady still staying with me after I continually take things out the house? These are items that she has worked for. I'm not working or helping to pay the bills. I had a nerve to take TVs and stereos out the house. I took her son's games and toys out the house like it was nothing to me. I knew it was wrong. I felt bad and I felt guilty about it, but I couldn't help it. It was like something took over me. It was a demon, or a monster, but I was the monster. I had a friend named Tony that I met on one of my jail visits. He was from Richmond, and he had a pickup truck. We would go out and work odd jobs to get some money to buy cigarettes, crack, and beer. That was the way we lived until the money ran out. One day we came across an abandoned building. It used to be an auto parts store or a garage of some sort. It wasn't open so we climbed the fence to get inside of it. We would take brake pads, copper, and all sorts of other items. We'd go sell the goods. We came back two or three times. The last time, the police showed up and we got arrested. I don't know what happened to Tony, but I know that I didn't get out on bond. And once again, I got sentenced to about 15 months in jail. I did my time in the jail and I went to a Regional Jail. I did excellent work there. I became a Teacher's Aide and a Worship Leader. Once again, I'm building up all these anticipations and hopes. Now, let's keep in mind that I haven't seen my son during any of this. He was now getting older and needs his father in his life. I've had no contact with his mother and then one day I got a visit. I didn't anticipate getting a visit at that time, but as I was standing waiting for my guest to come through, I became nervous, because it could be bad news like a death or something. When you are incarcerated, that's the last thing you want to hear. As I was staring through the glass with the phone to my head all I could see were women or parents coming to see other guys. They all walked past my section, when suddenly I saw a tall skinny young man who appeared to be about 13 or 14. He walked up, and I immediately recognized that it was my son. He grabbed the phone and just started to cry. It was one of the most touching things that I've ever experienced, because he was crying. He was crying because I was an absent father. He didn't know who I was, and he was a young black man who needed some guidance from the old black man who wasn't there. I didn't have guidance from my father, but with all his faults and issues that I used as an excuse, the one thing I can say about him is that I knew where he was. I grew up in the same household with my dad, but that is as far as it went with me. I'll give him that, but I won't give him anything else. Nevertheless, I was old enough that I needed to take personal responsibility for my own issues, and decisions. That young man standing in front of me on the other side of the glass only wanted somebody to stand there with him and be there for him. A man to help guide him. I wasn't that guy and I needed to be there for him. I was in and out of jails and prisons, smoking crack, getting high, chasing women, ripping, and running the streets. How in the hell am I going to be an example for him when I don't even know who I am. I needed him and he needed me, but I didn't know how to let him need me. I didn't know how to need him. That day when I left the visitors room, I vowed that I was going to be a better man, and a better father, but when I got out, that vow quickly ran into a snag. It wasn't because I didn't want to do it. What was it about me that made me put all my vows, promises, and hopes aside on release day? In my opinion, when most people get out of jails or prisons, they will pass a lie detector test.

Do you want to go back to jail? No and pass. Do you want to become a better person? Yes, and pass. Do you want to continue to do drugs and alcohol? No and pass, but something happens when we get out of jail and run into situations or circumstances that make us uncomfortable. We'd rather not deal with the pain, but we'd rather deal with old comfort zones that would lead us back to the same things that got us in trouble in the first place. So once again, I found myself building up a great outlook for my family only to have it torn down on top of my head and on the top of the heads of all those that loved me. All because I couldn't stop drinking and smoking crack. I always thought that I could control it. Maybe I could just drink on the weekends or during a game, but I couldn't. I couldn't drink at all, like I had an allergy to alcohol. Every time I drink, I'd break out. I'd break out in handcuffs. Yes, like you guessed, I got locked up again. It all became a regular part of life my. I was starting to accept the fact that I was just no good. I even went as far as saying that I'm worse than my father, except for the fact that I have never put my hands on a woman, ever! As far as everything else, I was miles apart from my father. As I told you in the past, every time I got locked up, I became a great citizen and extraordinary leader. Honestly, my skills as a teacher and preacher we're great, but only in prison. I could motivate a group of guys that wanted to fight each other in the prisons and put them together. I could encourage men to go out and do better, but when it came to me, I would get out jail and come back within a few months. There is no greater shame than to leave out of prison a great spiritual, Christian leader and then come back a few months as one of the biggest crack heads ever. I had to live that shame on multiple occasions, but this time when I came home, I gave myself a chance.

# PREACHER

I was released from jail again, this time around 2001. I had a different drive and desire, but this time I actually make an effort to change some things by going outside of my comfort zones. I also tried talking to some people that I normally wouldn't have spoken with. I went to AA meetings and attended church. My wife belonged to a church called the Morning Star in the South-Side of Richmond. It was a great church and more traditional as I liked. Everybody there knew my struggles, but this particular time, I approached the pastor and told him that I had a particular skill set and that I had a desire to be a minister. I thought that I was supposed to be a minister. Why not? I can speak well, memorize scripture, and I had a story to tell. I thought that was enough for me to be in the ministry. He allowed me the opportunity to become a minister in the church. That gave me a great source of pride. It also gave me a great obligation to my family and for those who were watching. I even obtained a full-time job after going to the temp service on a regular basis. I got hired by the Chesapeake Bay Cabinet Company. It was a small family-oriented company that made cabinets and delivered them to different job sites that were building new houses. I was very proud to have that job, and it was my first full-time job with benefits that I had in a long time. The whole staff loved me. The boss was very fond of me. He knew of my past and all the present things that I wanted to do. He helped me to get my license back, bought a car and told me that I didn't have to pay him back. His son loved me as if I was his own brother. I really had a good situation going on at work and church was going well. I started going to school at the Richmond Virginia Seminary to study more Christian philosophies. I also went to nursing homes to share my testimony and the gospel. It appeared that all was going well for me, and that I was using my past to better my future. Even my wife was very proud of me. She had seen the pains, the destruction, and the lies. She has seen me steal out the house, her wallet and I continued to ask her for money. She has seen me go back and forth to jail and now I am a minister. Now I am a student, a volunteer, a hard worker, and a taxpayer. I have become more responsible and I even made efforts to reconnect with my son. It seemed that things are going well. My stepson eventually came home from the military and things did not go well. He did not know the new person that I was trying to be and hell, to be honest, I didn't even know him myself. I did not know how to communication with him. I didn't know how to be this preaching husband nor be what everyone said I was supposed to be. I did not know how to navigate my home or apologize for the pain that I had caused them both in the past. Although they were proud of my accomplishments, it did not necessarily mean that they were supposed to do what I wanted them to do, especially him. He was a young, bright, and handsome man. It was just them two for many years and I come along and cause all this confusion. Now I can say that he was spoiled. Maybe he would admit it, or maybe she would, but things did not go well from time to time. Now, I am not talking about when I was drinking and drugging, but when I was doing well, which was not often. All sorts of people outside of the home were happy and respectful to this person I was trying to become. There were times I did not feel like being this good person when I was at home. Many times, I felt that I had caused too much damage to earn any respect or maybe I had not allowed them enough time to show me respect. It was just an uncomfortable situation, because I was just trying to learn how to be a man and I had allowed this new position in the community to dictate who I am instead of allowing God to dictate who I am. I realized that I was being selfish even though I was not drinking or smoking crack. I was still being selfish, because I wanted to do certain things in order for people to like and except me. While seeking their attention, I was still functioning in selfishness and it would soon manifest for everyone to see. At one of the local nursing homes that I visited every Thursday evening, a nurse there loved when I came by. She would always bring the residents down and then she would participate in the service. I kind of felt that she liked me. One evening I went upstairs with her on the elevator to get the other residents and she told me how nice and kind she thought that I was. She told me how she wanted a man just like me and how my wife was a lucky woman. Once again being the selfish individual that I was, I loved to hear that. I wanted to hear that I'm the great one. Now you have to understand this is a guy who spent years and years in and out of jail, running the streets, looking horrific

I was skinny, broke, and dirty and now I'm receiving all this attention from the ladies. I loved it. I enjoyed it. It fed my ego like nothing else. Do you know what it felt like to have a woman tell me how nice, sexy, and handsome I am? It did not matter how the woman looked or how she was built. The only thing that mattered was that she said it, and I was getting the attention. That's what I was desiring, and that was my new drug. I didn't know it at first until she gave me a call one early morning. I used to go to McDonald's every morning before work to get coffee and reflect. This particular morning, she called me and told me that her son was locked up. She didn't know what to do so I asked her to calm down and she just kept crying and crying. I told her that I was going to come over there to give her some help. I went over to my boss and told him the situation. I had so much favor at my job and they knew the work that I was doing in the community, so I could pretty much leave anytime I wanted to. So, I left, and I went over to her house. She opened up the door with a bathrobe on and it looked like she had been up all night. I tried to talk to her and console her. I told her some of my experiences dealing with the legal system. I also told her that her son has to get a bond and that the amount of money that they wanted for the bond wasn't the full amount. She only needed to pay 10%. That gave her a level of peace and it calmed her down, because she was able to pay the 10% to get her son out. She kept telling me how grateful she was that I came by and that she was tired of doing stuff by herself. She said that she needed someone to help and that she needed a man like me. She held my hand and stopped crying. She hugged me and the next thing you know we were kissing, and then soon after that we were making love to one another. The fire was lit, and it could not be put out. We went along with this relationship for about two or three months. It was really driving me crazy because I was not only trying to maintain the secrecy of this relationship, but I was also trying to manage my marriage; work a job, go to school, volunteer in the community and still be a minister. I was a walking contradiction, and it was driving me mad. I didn't have any peace and everything that was occurring in my life that was small, became a big thing. There was no way that I could tell anybody because of my selfishness.

I do not want anybody to think that I'm a bad person. I do not want you to think that I'm a hypocrite. I didn't want anyone to think that I'm a cheater. I want you to think that I am the greatest thing since Jesus, because I'm selfish and that's all that matters right now. So, when I didn't leave my wife, as she wanted me to, she just left me alone, but that just opened the door for other women. This one particular woman lived right across the street from the church. We had a relationship for about two weeks, but she really wanted me to leave my wife and when I didn't, she called the church and told some of the people about me. The pastor pulled me aside one day in the office and shared it with me.

He said, "I don't know what's going to happen, but there's one thing I do know. There are two things that will get you into trouble. One is lying to the people about money and the other is lying to the people."

Those words still ring true in my head today. Those very same words would come back to face that same pastor. Somehow, I managed to get through that phase without anyone knowing, so I thought. Although I was no longer having sex with other women I still desired too, and I still wanted too. By this time, I felt like my whole world was out of control. I didn't feel like I had any authority in life. I was trying to be a man and the whole problem was that I didn't know how to be one. I was trying to make my stepson do what I wanted him to do, because I was living a new life. I wanted him to go to church when I wanted him to go to church. I wanted my wife to support me by making my stepson do the things that I wanted him to do. All I did was add a lot of confusion and stress to my household. Any kind of peace that I might have had was no longer in the house. It was outside of the house. So, this is my life. I am just trying to manage, and be the big man outside of my home, all the while, I'm feeling like a little man inside. I'm just trying to go through the motions without doing drugs or drinking. It's been a couple years since I had anything to drink, smoke or get high, but other than that there's not a lot to cheer about. Even though I have many people who think I'm the greatest of all time or am I just telling myself that. There would soon come a situation that will rock my already fragile foundation.

On Palm Sunday, during Easter of 2003, the Pastor didn't show up. The Assistant Pastor performed the service and the people went on throughout the week as if nothing was wrong. So, we had Holy Night Services every night that week and the Pastor didn't show up to any of the services, which was odd. So, when Easter Sunday came, no one knew where the Pastor was. Now let's remember, I'm an Associate Pastor I sit up in the pulpit with the other Ministers. I had no idea what happened to Pastor, and no one was speaking about it. So later on, that week, everybody found out that we were going to have a church meeting. It seems that the Pastor has some issues, and we had a church meeting that Saturday. The Pastor and his wife were both present. He got up to address the church and to share with us why he wasn't available the past couple of weeks. He told us that he had been detained, in other words he had been arrested. He told us that it was for a DUI and that he had a drinking issue to deal with. He prays that we would continue to allow him to be Pastor. He was sorry for any trouble or inconvenience that he might have caused the congregation.

Then he said, "Now, my wife and I are going to go out and have something to eat. We're going to leave you to your business of voting."

He grabbed his wife by the arm and she forcibly snatched her arm away and went up to the mic very angrily and said, "My husband has been here for a lot of years and he has seen so much dirt, trouble and lies. How dare you even consider removing my husband?"

He was trying to grab her by the arm and pull her away

She said, "No, I'm going to say this!! My husband has been there for everybody, and for you to turn your back on him right now just isn't right."

She said some other things that I won't dare repeat, but she finally finishes her peace and the Pastor, and the First Lady walked out of the church, like a great battle had just been won. So, the Church had the vote and the majority of the church decided that they wanted to keep the Pastor. As I was looked around the pulpit, I was the only Minister that voted to keep the pastor.

That didn't sit well with me, because I already felt like an outsider. So, it was decided, the Church was going to keep its Pastor. After all, how can we preach forgiveness if we don't forgive one of our own? To earn back his respect, he had to put some work in. Now let's remember, I'm already going through my own little contradictions; multiple women, lying, cheating and deception. I really couldn't say anything and that's why it was easy for me to go for forgiveness. Later on, that week, I would get a call from the church secretary while I was at work. She was very upset and told her that I needed to hurry and go to the local Community Pride and get all the Free Press papers. I went and told my boss and they allow me to go. So, I went to the local Community Pride and got stacks and stacks of the local Free Press. I brought them back to the church and loaded them into the office. She quickly grabbed one of the papers and turned to a page and said, "Honey, who is this?"

As I looked at the paper, I saw two pictures; one of them was a picture of my Pastor with the suit on and the other picture was a lady beside him. The article was talking about a pastor who was arrested for prostituting. So, what I was looking at was a picture of my Pastor in drag and the other picture was him in his suit. My Pastor was arrested for prostituting him-self. This was a blow that was surely going to destroy the church. The first thing I did was go home. I took a paper with me to show my wife who had been a longtime member of this church. She loved that Pastor. Hell, many people loved him. I loved him because he gave me an opportunity to serve in the church, but you couldn't ignore this, and all the while, I'm thinking about my own stuff that I'm going through. That Saturday, we were supposed to go to the Hamptons Ministers Conference. I drove the church van to Hampton University for the conference. We went down for that one day. Everyone knew who my Pastor was, and they also knew his father, who was from Atlanta. They were very popular in the Southern Baptist Community. They both had multiple degrees in education. Everyone in attendance knew who he was, and I said to myself, there's no way my Pastor was going to come to this event. He eventually showed up towards the end of the day. I watched as he managed to go through the crowds of people that he has known for years and decades. Pastors, ministers, and teachers; all talked with him about his situation. There was no way I would have attended that event, but I'm a runner. He managed to get through the day and as we were about to embark on our journey home. The Pastor decided that he was going to ride back with us. The lines to get out the parking lot were so long that we asked the ladies to wait on the side of the curb while the Pastor and I walked to get the van. While we were in the van waiting for the traffic to die down, I had the opportunity to talk to the pastor like I wanted to without being confined to any religious restrictions. It was just two men being real with one another other.

I simply asked him, "Hey brother, was that you in that picture?"

He said, "Yeah Rev. Duke, that's me."

Then I asked, "What are you going to do about it?"

He said, "I don't know!"

I said, "Well brother, whatever you do I love you man. I appreciate you and I just pray that God will give you the right direction to follow, because I remember when you told me there are two things that'll get you in trouble. One is lying to the people about money and the other is lying to the people."

He had some decisions to make, but the church was going to help him make that decision. We finally had a church meeting and decided that the pastor had to go. It caused a great split in the church. It was nothing that we could do because he lied to us. If he would have told us that he had issues, sexual issues, from the first meeting, maybe there was a possibility that he could have stayed in some capacity, but not as Pastor. There was nothing that could be done, because he had lied directly to the people and the pain from that situation was so great that many people couldn't get past it. The church split and the people were arguing about which direction to go and how they should explore finding a new pastor. Many fingers were pointing at me to become Pastor of the Church. They thought I was a young, intelligent, and fresh face to lead the church. I had a testimony in which I came out of some stuff. My wife loved the church and they love her. They also loved how I preached, but I was still feeling guilty about the stuff that I had done in the past while being a minister. In my opinion my home was a wreck. How can I be an example to a church when I can't be an example in my home? I'm not saying that the people in my house are evil, but it just felt like I wasn't being respected. I felt like I should have been respected. I have far too many arguments with my wife and my stepson over things that you should never have arguments about in the first place. Plus, I wasn't living right. So, I had a meeting with the church leaders. I knew they wanted to talk to me about possibly being a pastor. I did want to hear the idea of it, but I was scared of what it might entail and all the responsibility that came with it. I wasn't living right, and I had not yet come to terms with what I had done, but I was going, nevertheless. When I arrived at the meeting, they asked me all types of uncomfortable questions like, do feel any sexual attraction to the pastor? What makes us think that you won't go back to prison again? Do you ever have any desires to get high? Do you have any desire for children sexually? This type of questioning went on and on. I was so angry that I said to myself, who do they think they are talking to? What makes these people think that they have the right to ask me questions like this? They don't know me! I don't know what they're fucking doing. The questions just kept coming and coming and they finally said, "Thank you for your time! We will get back with you in the future."

I left and my anger drove me to the store. I have not had a drink in about three or four years. I grabbed me a 40 ounce of Colt 45 and put it on the counter. I knew if I drank this that I was going to have an issue. Nevertheless, I popped it open and I drunk the whole 40 ounces at one time. I sat in the car with all the Bible tracks, and gospel CDs in my seat. I did not play a single song. I allowed the guilt to consume me and I kept drinking and drinking. In a couple of days, I was smoking crack. No one knew where I was, and no one had seen me for days. I have completely lost my mind. I sold my car, I lost my job, and I've been on the streets for weeks. Now I'm back on the streets homeless, hanging on the corners with alcoholics and drunks. I went from the pulpit to the gutter in a matter of hours and days. I didn't care about anything, and the guilt was forcing me to stay away. Once again, my selfishness didn't allow me to talk to anyone, because I was more concerned about what someone would think about me rather than being concerned about what's the next best move to make. I was back in the gutter again.

After about a good month and a half of running the streets, I finally decided to call home. I had lost everything; my car, job and my dignity was gone. The only things that I had left were pain, shame, and guilt, which were very good friends of mine. I decided to call my wife who was very angry, but she was happy to hear from me because she didn't know if I was dead or alive, like many other times before. I told her how tired I was, and I just wanted to come home. She wanted me to come home, but she said that she needed to tell me something. A couple of weeks prior to me calling, the church had tried to communicate with her to try to find out where I was. It seems to me that there was a serious discussion about me becoming the next pastor of the church. One thing that I believe is that God has revealed to me that I was not ready to become anyone's pastor. That church had already been through hell from the first incident. There was no way they needed or deserved to be put through the hell that I would put them through. It was also revealed to me the ease of how we can allow the enemy to creep in and steal things right before our blessing. I wasn't prepared to be a pastor, lead a congregation of people or be their moral compass, simply because I didn't have one. I didn't understand what it was even though I had a whole library of information stored in my head about biblical precepts and concepts. Hebrew and Greek commentary on all of these things did not stop me from living in shame again, because of what could have been. It was lost once again because of drugs and alcohol. So, I made my way home to face the music. I couldn't get my job back or my position at the church. All was gone and once again I took solace in my pain. I went directly back to my old habits of drinking and smoking crack. It wasn't long before I found myself back on the streets again, staying days at a time, sleeping in abandoned cars and houses. I ate wherever I could. This occurred, not because I didn't have a place to go, but because I was in too much pain. I didn't have any peace in my home and that was a manifestation of what I didn't have in my heart and in my life. I checked into a local hospital which is something that I did frequently. Every time I stayed out longer than I wanted to, or I didn't want to come home, I would just call 911 and tell them that I am suicidal. I would try and force them to take me to one of the local hospitals so I could get a couple of days rest. I abused that privilege so many times, but on this particular time they offered me some help. After having a serious conversation with my wife and other people, I decided to go Arizona. My wife didn't really understand why I wanted to go to Arizona, but deep down inside I wanted to run. I wanted to get away. I thought that running from Portsmouth and Richmond was going to solve my problems. I thought that if I left and went to a faraway place that all her problems with me would go away and my problems with her would go away. It seemed like everything I touch gets destroyed. I needed to leave! I needed to leave Virginia all together, so I made my decision to go to Arizona.

# ARIZONA

After spending the night with my wife and being in the state of mind that I was in it was easy to tell that I needed some help. I needed to do something, or I was going to die. I boarded the Greyhound bus the next morning and headed to Arizona on a three-day journey. The bus trip was very bad on me because I didn't have anything. All I had was enough money to eat, but I used that drinking on the bus, so I didn't eat. I had to borrow money from passengers or inside of bus stops whenever we would stop. I did meet this lady who carried liquor with her from New Orleans and man did we get drunk. I had fun with her on the bus trip. She finally was dropped off in New Mexico and I was alone again, but I did get a chance to experience something that I never experienced before. At about 3 a.m. I woke up in El Paso and I remembered seeing some men with badges walking down the aisle asking everybody for IDs. He got to me and walked past. I couldn't understand why, but I was starting to wake up a little more and when he got off the bus, I noticed that everybody on the bus appeared to be Mexican. I was the only black person on the bus. There wasn't even a white person on the bus and then it dawned on me that those people were probably Border Patrol. That was a new experience to me. In the Southwest, there weren't many black people around, but there were plenty of Mexican, Native Americans and Whites. Blacks were rare and being from Richmond, Virginia, that was a culture shock. When I finally arrived in Mesa, Arizona, I went into this drug program. They came to pick me up from the Greyhound Bus Station. As soon as I got there, I didn't like it. It was about 80 people there and I was one of four black men. Everybody had issues with drugs, and alcohol, but in Arizona, they had an issue that I wasn’t aware of; it was called meth. Meth was a monster, and it was destroying people. Arizona was just a weird place and it stayed warm all the time, but I loved the heat. My first week in the program my old boss sent me some money to help me get cosmetics and to get myself situated. I remember asking for permission to go to the store so that I could buy some cosmetics, and when I got to the store, I noticed that there was a young white guy standing on the corner. He nodded his head to me, and I nodded back.

Even though I wasn't from Arizona, it wasn't hard for me to tell that he was trying to tell me something. I thought he had some drugs, because we drug addicts just recognize certain things. So, I went into the store and bought me a beer, (yes, I'm fucking up already all the way in Arizona) and when I came out the guy asked, "What's up?"

He showed me a whole bag of crack. Then he asked, "What do you need man? I got you."

My eyes immediately lit up and all the pain that I went through, all the lies that I told, all the promises that I made, again once, went out the window. I bought me a $20 piece from him, and went inside the store. I got me a can of soda, went behind one of the buildings in Arizona, and got high. I repeated this until all my money was gone. Later on, that night, I did not have any money and I did not have anywhere to sleep in a place I have never been before. I am too ashamed to go back to program, so I chose to stay out on the streets of Mesa, Arizona. Now I have been homeless on the streets for about a week, going back and forth meeting homeless people and hanging out with Native Americans. We were drinking and beer getting high and one day I saw some men working on a roof. They asked me how I was doing, and they told me they were in a program, and they would love to have me. They said they would give me a ride to the program tomorrow if I wanted to come. I took them up on their offer and I went back with them to Phoenix, Arizona. It was a Christian program, so I was sort of comfortable with it. I was the only black person in the program. The program was run by a church and I was the only black in the congregation. Over a few days, these people came to love me. When they found out that I was able to teach scripture, preach and sing with all my other talents, they allowed me to teach Bible study and Sunday school to their children. Can you imagine this young black man teaching Sunday school to all these little White, Native American, and Mexican kids? They trusted me with their children and was I was very good at what I did. My heart just wasn't right. I really, really, really, tried! I gave them ideas on how to bring more people into the church and my thoughts about Outreach. I also stated how to make a bigger impact on the community, and they all listened attentively.

I even got a job with one of the local telemarketing companies, making phone calls for handicapped veterans. It was a great job for me, because I liked to talk anyway. So, things were going very well for me in Arizona, but once again my demons showed up. I called home and I told my wife about the beautiful situation and how excited I was to have a new job and how God was moving in my life. I wanted her to move to Arizona, but my wife wasn't comfortable with that situation, and for good reason. So, my wife and I got into a very heated conversation about how she didn't want to come to Arizona. My point was that we are married, things are happening for me here. You know I have challenges and a history back in Virginia. So, this is a new beginning and a new chance for both of us, but she didn't see it that way. She has family that she wanted to be near and she didn't know if she should upload everything and come live in Arizona, just to see me destroy everything again. Frankly, she had every right to think that, because history would indicate that I would do it again. So, we went back and forth, and I got discouraged and I told her that I would talk to her later. I wasn't ready to come home because things are going too well for me here. A couple of hours later the Pastor of the church called me into his office and tells me of a phone call that he received from my wife. First of all, before he said anything else, I was already highly upset because the one thing that my wife knows is how I feel about people sharing my personal information. Here I am, in a whole other state and she has made a phone call to a man who she has never met before, telling him some very personal and intimate details about our marriage. That is exactly what happened. He told me that what was going on between my wife and I was none of his business. He said he still loves me and supports me if I wanted to stay there and be a part of the Ministry. So, his comforting words did not help me any, because I was so infuriated. I was so consumed with anger and the audacity of my wife calling and telling that man my personal and private things; like, how I keep going back and forth to prison. How I lied and how I stole things out of the house. She was telling him the truth, but the question and the fact of the matter is why did she have to tell him in that first place? Nevertheless, I left the office and I went to the dormitory where all the guys are staying.

I told them I'll be back, and that needed to get some air. So, I left the church site as pissed off as I could be. I left Jesus, the Bible, my spiritual principles, and faith all behind me that particular day. I walked to the one of the local corner stores, went to the cooler and got a 24 ounce can of beer; Bull to be exact. I went to a bus stop, sat down and just wondered what I was about to do. Once again, I was about to throw away any hope that I have built up in myself and among other people with one can of beer. Nevertheless, my selfishness took over as it normally does. I popped open the can of beer and I drunk it all in a couple of gulps. As I sat at the bus stop, one of the buses pulled up. I didn't have anything else to do so I got on the bus and rode to see the streets of Phoenix. It didn't take long for me to recognize some familiar spots. Like I said, a drug addict can just recognize certain things about city. About a mile or so down the road, the bus drove past a park. The park was full of people, hanging out, and playing basketball. Others were hanging out on the corners under the shelters. Girls, guys, whites, blacks, young and old were all there. I had to get off the bus so I could see what I can find. I had about $200 in my pocket, and my first thought was to find out who has the crack. As I was walking around, I noticed that people were looking at me funny; not only because I was black, but because I was very muscular at that time. I spent three months in the program and all I really did was eat and lift weights. I didn't really pay any mind to how muscular I have gotten, but people thought I was the police. I have been accused of many things in my past, but one thing I was never accused of was being the Police. So, a Black bald-headed man, in shape, was something that wasn't ordinary on the streets of Phoenix, Arizona, but someone eventually took a chance and sold me something. I didn't know what to do so I bought a dime of crack. I thought the guy sold me a dummy, because what he gave me was so big. I found out that it was the regular size in Phoenix, because of the close nature to the Border. The drugs were plentiful and that became a bigger problem since I was a strange face, with a strange sense of humor, a few muscles, and a few dollars in my pocket. I gained a lot of attention from the girls out in the park.

The white girls, Mexican girls, black girls, and the Native American girls. Now there's one thing about crack. Even though I had a desire to do whatever I wanted to do with all of those girls, crack killed my drive. They were willing to give me sex or oral sex outside at any time, but the crack was always an enemy of mine. It never allowed me to keep an erection so any girl that hung around me knew that all she had to do was talk enough stuff and rub me a little bit and they're going to get high and not have to worry about giving me any sex. The old boy could not perform while smoking crack, but that didn't stop me. It wasn't long before all my money was gone and, once again, I'm too ashamed to go back to the program. Now this park was no joke and I was hanging out there. No one knew me and Arizona is a very racist place, but I managed and learned how to navigate the streets. I learned how to panhandle, and I hung around certain bums and winos. I went from group to group for acceptance. I would do whatever I needed to do to fit in. I got drunk with the Native Americans, smoked weed around the Mexicans, and smoked crack with the white boys, because, being black, I was the odd man out. Homelessness in Arizona was at a whole other level because of how warm it is year-round. A person can be homeless in Arizona and spend his or her spend whole life in that condition but being homeless anywhere else was never easy. It has been one the most challenging things I have ever done, especially because I didn't have to be out there. It was always the guilt that was driving and keeping me out there. I would wake up and try to find something to drink just to deal with the guilt. I would also try to steal something to get money for crack, just to deal with the guilt. One morning around 7 a.m., a possible answer came when I was outside one of the local Home Depots. I was trying to pan-handle enough money to get something to drink, because I was really a terrible alcoholic. I couldn't function unless I had something to drink. So, as I was standing by the door, a white gentleman walked up and asked, "How are you doing today sir?"

I said, "Fine sir! Would you happen to have some spare change so I can get me something to eat?"

He said, "Let me go into the store and I'll check you out when I come out."

When he comes out of the store, he was hauling a bunch of sheetrock in a cart.

He told me if I helped him put the sheetrock in the car that he'll give me a few dollars.

I said, "Okay, thank you!"

We walked over to his car and we loaded the sheetrock in the car. When we were finished loading the sheetrock, we had a brief conversation. He asked me where I was from and what was my name was? He also asked what was I doing out here? I told him my name, where I was from and that I got caught up on drugs. I said I was running away from certain situations and I didn't really have anywhere to go. I've been here for about six months.

He asked, "Do you want to go home?"

I said, "I would love to go home!"

He said, "Well, how much does it cost to get home?"

I said, "Well, on the Greyhound, it costs maybe $185 dollars. It is a 3-day trip and I just can't get that type of money right now."

He went into his wallet whipped out three $100 bills and gave them to me and said, "Go home!"

I looked at this man and all I could do was cry. I gave him a hug and we talked awhile. I thanked him over and over again. He gave me the money to be able to go home, and he didn't have to do that. He didn't know me from Adam, so I walked over to the store and got my beer. I sat down and contemplated a bit. Then I headed back to the park instead of going home or preparing myself to go home. I did what I normally had done in the past. I disregarded all judgement and wisdom and found the crack man. I located some of my friends and some girls and splurged. All that money was smoked up in a few hours and I was left alone again. I was a little bit more hungrier, a little skinnier, a little bit more angrier, and a little bit more guiltier.

How could I allow that to happen? I wanted people to love me so much that I would just spend all my money to have someone stand around me and tell me what a great guy that I am. That's all well and good until the money's gone and then you're all alone again. So, I lived my life like that for a few more weeks, then the same church that I left came up to the park to do Outreach. I felt so bad and embarrassed that I didn't know what to do. Those people looked at me and embrace me. They did not judge me. They showed me love. It is amazing how love can impact a person when it is applied in the right way. Sometimes we think that we are doing the right thing by judging and placing condemnations on people. These are the very same tools that are used to keep a person in the same condition that they're trying to get out of. The power of love can be a life-changing weapon. So, they asked me to come back with them and I did. The healing was to start again, but I was too far gone. I was able to go back to my job at the telemarketer. I would work for a couple of weeks to get a paycheck and then I was gone again, this time not to return. I knew the city a little better, so I decided to explore some different places. One of the places that I hung out for a long time was 24th and Indian School in Phoenix, Arizona. I can't tell you how I ended up there, but I was able to find certain homeless people, hang out with them and drink all day, but when I met this guy named Cowboy and his girlfriend, Jennifer, things went to another level for me. Cowboy was a wild child. He was a tall, skinny and a total redneck. He thought I was the coolest brother he ever met. A lot of that, I guess was because, I had an East Coast mentality about me. It wasn't about the racial mentality that Phoenix tended to carry. I normally spoke my mind on a multitude a subjects. Nobody on the streets of Arizona knew that I was a licensed ordained minister. No one knew that I could read and speak a little Greek and Hebrew. None of them knew that I was big on politics, history and that I loved multiple types of music. All they knew was that I was an alcoholic, crack head and a guy struggling on the streets trying to get a hit of crack every once in a while. Cowboy and I were cool, and Jennifer his girlfriend, was just someone there to say yes to him. I think she was kind of a trophy for him.

She was a real skinny blonde girl and a total alcoholic. She didn't smoke crack. They went everywhere together. Cowboy knew that I was by myself and that I didn't know anybody out there so he would let me come into his outside camp and sleep because there's always safety in numbers. I respected and I appreciated that because it means something to be able to go to sleep in peace. I really couldn't do that because Cowboy was so damn crazy. He could snap on me at any given minute and he always carried a knife with him. At the drop of a dime, he'd be ready to rob somebody. It didn't matter if they were in a wheelchair or if they were young or old. He had this one lick that he would always do. He would ask me if I wanted to walk with him to the corner store and wait. He would go somewhere behind the store to a neighborhood. I believe it was some old gentleman that he was going to visit and every time. He would bring back $60 or $75. I found out that he was going in and taking money from this man. I don't know what he was doing or how he was doing it. All he wanted me to do was wait for him at the store, and when he came back, we would go get some crack and get some beer. Afterward, we would come back to the campsite and do it again if we had enough time throughout the day. So that was my life for a couple of months, hanging out with Cowboy and Jennifer. Sometimes Cowboy would leave Jennifer and I and go make some money on his own. Cowboy was just a free child. So, there would be many times that I was left alone with this drunk white girl. Jennifer was so scared of me that she didn't know what to say or do. I would have tried her, but I was in Arizona and I didn't need any white woman to say that I was trying to take advantage of her, so I never did. She passed multiple looks during the days and times that we were together. She would also make slick side comments like why they say black guys have big dicks. I would be very careful to watch my words. I would make a comment like, I don't know. I can't speak for everybody. I can only speak for myself and then I'd leave it alone, and she wouldn't go any further either. She was just testing me to see what I would do, but I will have more information on Jennifer later.

Eventually, Cowboy got locked up and Jennifer moved on to some other guy that was waiting in line and I found myself alone, hustling, and scrambling. I went to another spot of town on 24th and

Van Buren. Now this was my spot, and it was my home. I was near the food, airport, and crack. I was also near a hospital and I was near stores that I can go in and boost from them. I met multiple people like this guy named Al. He was a short, white haired, Caucasian boy. He would go to the local pornography shops, steal videos, and sex toys. We would go out and sell them for crack. He was an alcoholic and crackhead just like me. So, we hung out. He had a little place under the steps of a large corporation that was closed. You had to crawl underneath the steps to get to it, but once you got underneath of it, there was a lot of space. People would come under there to smoke, get high, trick, and go to sleep. It was the craziest thing I have ever seen in my life, but it was a part of my world. After you take a hit of crack under there it was like the Twilight Zone. In one corner there were people having sex, and in the other corner, people were shooting up, and in the other corner people were trying to sleep. All of this took place under the steps of a building. Every once in a while, I would check myself into a hospital and stay about 3 or 4 days, and come out again and do the same thing just like I did in Richmond, but now, I was starting to get more comfortable living in Arizona. I was starting to become familiar with the guys who were selling dope and the guys who were coming to pick it up. I learned who the boosters and tricks were. Everybody knew who I was. I was often the only black guy out there and people took advantage of me a lot. Some people didn't respect me by not giving me my drugs when I paid for them or they would call me nigger. I had to bite my tongue on a lot of things because I was alone. The girls would get together for tricking and asked me to come and stay with them so they could have somebody with them for protection. Hell, who was I going to protect? All of them loved me, but none of them wanted to have sex with me. They all kept telling me that I didn't belong out there, and that I needed to go home. Deep down inside, I knew that they were right, because everywhere I went, I just didn't feel comfortable, but here I am. Plus, I didn't know many women. Regardless of the condition that they were in they wouldn't have had sex with me, and at my best, I was 5 feet 11 inches, 130 pounds and 5 shades darker. I looked like death, but the ride would never stop.

While I was at the store one day, I saw one of the guys who used to be in the program with me at the church. He wasn't looking too good. He looked like he had relapsed. He asked me did I know where anything was, and I told him yeah. So, we went to go get beer, crack, and then he got a room. He kept asking me if I knew where the girls were at and I said yeah. Now some people react differently when they smoke crack. I can't be still. I have to walk or something. This guy, he wanted girls in the room just to look at him. He'll take a hit of crack, while on the toilet, pull his penis out, and start playing with. He would twist his mouth like he was chewing gum. He didn't want the girls to do anything, just to look at him. Now, I didn't feel like standing there watching this guy play with his penis, and I couldn't have sex with any of the girls because I was smoking crack. So, I just sat around waiting for my next hit. He asked me to go get some more crack. He gave me about $145 to $200 and let me use his van. So, I went to go find some crack, and I decided to test it before I got back. One of the girls that I knew went with me, and she took a few hits in the van. The next thing you know, I was driving the van all night. I never returned it. I kept the van and drove all over the city getting high; struggling to get gas and food. I was able to sleep in it and other people were able to sleep in it also. I was all over the place without any regard for the guy whose van it was, the police, or any family that might have been looking for it. I just didn't care. I was just riding through the streets of Arizona taking people to go steal, buy drugs, and all kinds of stuff. I even let girls prostitute in the van. I was a Chauffeur. I'm not exerting any skills, but people need me because they want transportation. There were many times I contemplated taking the van back and just drop it off at the program and let it sit, but that was my way to obtain crack. It was my way to obtain money, and it was my way of being important. I needed to be important, so I held on to the van for as long as I could. At one of the local stores I saw the white girl Jennifer again. She was with her new boyfriend. He was a white dude who went to work on odd jobs. He was homeless, but he would take his money and spend it on Jennifer. They wanted to hang out and ride around. He would buy gas and beer, but he wouldn't smoke crack.

He took a lot of my time up that I would normally use for chasing crack. Nevertheless, I didn't have anything else to do so I would drink beer with them all day long. One day he asked me if I would take him to work. The next morning he said he would give me $150. He had a job somewhere in Mesa and I agreed. He didn't have any money then, but I would have to drop him off that night so he can work. Jennifer and I would have to find a place to stay, so I agree to the terms. We drove to Mesa and dropped him off at work. That night, Jennifer and I just rode around for a few hours trying to get something to drink. We were able to hustle up enough money to get us a 12-pack and drove to one of the empty areas of the desert in Mesa. I parked the van and we started drinking. We started talking about the last time we seen each other and how Cowboy was doing. She told me that he had got really sick and that she misses him, but she has to do what she has to do. She told me how good I looked. I knew that was a lie, but I sucked it up because I knew where this was going. It looked like I was going to finally get Jennifer. She kept saying to me that we can't do anything, but after a few beers, we were having sex in the desert like wild animals, and it was good. It was the conquering of the white woman, and I gave her every reason to remember a black man. Now we were in a strange van in the middle of the open desert at night, and the police came and asked me what we were doing out here in the desert. I was scared to death knowing that I was with this white woman all by myself in a stolen van. Plus, I didn't have a driver's license and I was drunk. So, we just simply told them the story of her friend going to work and we didn't have a place to sleep.

It was only by God's grace that the Officer said, "You have to find another place to sleep."

He let us go and we went to one of the gas stations where we saw a drive-thru car wash and parked there until the morning. When her boyfriend came out, he did as he said. He gave me the money, and I took them to a hotel. I then went on about my business. I hung out with this black girl for a while who was just as much of a con artist as I was. One day I went to the bathroom and she pulled off in the van.

She did the very exact thing that I had done to many people and it didn't feel good. I wanted to kill her and then I thought about it. I wondered how people felt when I took their vehicles. I mean this is not a piece of crack, it was a car. I mean we're talking about thousands of dollars. This was potentially someone's livelihood and I have done this to people on multiple occasions, and this time it happened to me. So, with a little courage, I found my way back to 24th and Van Buren. I never saw the guy whose van that I took, but if I did see him, I wanted him to forgive me so that we could go back to our regular order of business, getting high, and smoking crack.

24th and Van Buren was my home. People would always come around who did crack and that was the way I hustled; sell it, buy it, and smoke it. There were different people who came around to score from different people. I had my own little group of people. When they wanted something, I would go and make a phone call and the guy would come back and bring me some dope. He would give me something for the selling it and the people that I scored for would give me something. That's how I maintained for months. There was one day that something happened very strange, and I happened to be out there all alone. People were coming to me for drugs all that day, and I was the only one out there. Then this gay guy comes around looking for his peeps.

So, I asked him, "What's up brother? What do you need?"

He said, "I need some crack."

He wanted to go get a 20, so I told him, if you hold on for a minute I'll make a phone call, but he won't come for $20. The guy told me he had $40. So, I made the phone call, and nothing happened. Now let's keep in mind that I did not know that this gentleman was gay at the time so I told him I know a place where we can go around the corner. I got in the car with him. It was a nice car. It was a jet black, two door, sports car, and it looked brand new. It only had enough room for two people. So, we went to the house and he gave me the $40. I went in the house and I came out with the drugs.

We then drove around the corner so he could test it. He put a hit on his pipe, and I put one hit on mine, and we both took a blast, and here come the questions.

"Do you like to party dude?"

"What do you mean, do I like to party bro?"

I already saw what was coming, because I've been out in the streets long enough to recognize it. I just wanted him to say it. So, he put another piece on his pipe and I put another piece on mine. We took another hit of the crack until was gone. He wanted some more so he whipped out his wallet and pulled out about $800. My eyes got big and my voice went immediately from having bass to high pitch, trying to sound like I'm gay. It was a part of my crack head skills to become whatever I needed to get what I wanted. So, I let him think that I was down with the program.

In a pitiful gay voice, I said, "How much do you want?"

Now imagine me saying that like a gay guy. One thing about an addict is that we know how to be a chameleon. We can conform to any role, because we are good actors. So I took the $800 and I went in the house and we bought all the crack that the dealer had. He was trying to get me to go back to his house, and I kept telling him that I can't go, because we got to get our head right first. So, we just kept smoking crack and he kept buying alcohol. It was a perfect day for me as long as I was in the car. I didn't have to feed into anything, and I didn't have to do anything I didn't want to do. All that I had do was keep lying, which was my M.O. We went all night, getting high and drinking in the car until all the crack was gone. I told him if we had some more money, we could go get a room and we can stay there for the rest of the day. I'm just trying to get him to go get some more money. So, we drove to his apartment complex in the West End of Phoenix. This place was beautiful, and it was gated. I was nervous being on those grounds. He told me that he can't go in his apartment looking like this.

He was paranoid and he had spent over $800. He didn't know what to do, but this fool actually gave me the keys to his apartment and told me the directions to get there. He gave me instructions to open up a little box that has some money in it.

He said, "Get two $100 bills out."

I looked at him and I said, "Are you sure?"

I was trying to sound like I was very concerned about his well-being.

He said, "Yeah man, you're good. You're cool! Just get $200, and come back."

I did as he asked, and I went to his room. I was also paranoid because I was a black man in this housing complex and people were looking at me like I was crazy. This had to be around 11 o'clock in the morning. I used the key to open the door and I followed the directions that he gave me. It led me to a jewelry box that was in his bedroom. I open it up to find eleven $100 bills. My instructions were to grab two $100 bills, leave the rest, and come back. Now, I wasn't that good at following instructions. I actually took all of the money and put it in my pocket. I closed the door, locked it, and went the opposite way of where his car was parked. I just walked through the apartment complex and kept walking until I found myself at a store, and I called a cab. I hid and ran from this gentleman for the longest time. People even told me that Mafia type people were looking for me, but I didn't care. I was gone, and I had to have it.

I stayed away from 24th and Van Buren for about 2 months, but I eventually ended up back there. It didn't really make a difference to me at that time. I was on the verge of death and I didn't have any hope or pride. I felt my life was over. I gave up, but there was more crack to smoke. There was a Latino couple named Ramos and Irma. They were like the royalty of the streets. They weren't doing anything specific or spectacular, they were just trying to survive. He was a true hustler and she was too. Irma liked me when we first met, because this was one of the times I came out of the hospital. She would always flirt with me, but Ramos and I were really cool with one another other. He had other women who wanted to get with him because of the activities that he was involved with. He wasn't a bad looking dude either. I believe the money made him more attractive to some women. I was always in and out of their graces, mainly, because of her, but when I had those vehicles, they were always close to me, because I could take them places. All I needed from them was a little bit of coke here and there. The months and months of the street life allowed them to get to know me. Ramos found an abandoned house and got someone to cut the power on. There were many people who stayed there; most of them were girls who were tricking, and guys like me who were close to them and helped to watch out. So, we were are living in an abandoned house that had lights and running water. It is funny what a little crack can do. On New Year's Eve, 2004, we found ourselves doing the usual. We were trying get drunk and get high.

Even Irma said to me, “Duke all you want to do is drink.”

But the shame of what had come out her mouth to me didn’t stop me from drinking until I passed out like I normally do around 2 or 3 in the evening, when everything and everyone are completely up. I woke up around 10 p.m. the night of New Year's Eve, and I needed a beer really bad, but I couldn't find one. All I saw were the women. All the guys were gone out doing their thing and I was the only one there around eight or nine women. I noticed that they were all talking about their life. What they would do better, and what the New Year could bring. I sat there and pondered my situation as well and I realized that they were all crying. That did something to me. That spirit that was dead in me awakened. The encourager, motivator, and preacher came forth. Although I looked like death and I was, it was safe to say that I knew that God was about to do something. So, I got up off the couch and dusted myself off. It was approaching midnight and I was still the only guy in the house. I just simply asked all the women to come to the kitchen and that I wanted to say something, and everybody came. We all stood in a circle and I told them about my life, and my past struggles. I told them about how I ended up at this point and I asked them if I can say a little prayer for our families, children, and our future. Everyone agreed so I prayed, and I let it out. That power came out of me just like it has so many times before and you could hear the tears falling to the ground. You could hear the women gasping in pain as my voice would become more powerful and deeper. Gods Spirit cut through that house that night and when the clock struck twelve, everybody hugged each other, and I went back to the couch by myself. It felt like a great weight was lifted off me. Later on, that morning around 2 a.m., one of the girls came and sat down beside me. She was still kind of shaken from the prayer. She just looked at me with curiosity and wonder in her eyes.

She said, “Duke, what are you doing out here? You don't belong out here with us. You need to go home. Don't die out here with the rest of us. Duke you need to go home.”

She just walked off and left me feeling so empty and confused. I knew she was right, but I didn't have the courage to make the first step to making that happen. I haven't heard from my wife in months, and I missed my son so bad. That was the worst part of all. Even though I had never really spent any time with him. I'm in such bad physical, mental, and spiritual condition, who would want me back anyway? Why would I want to go back to Richmond or any part of Virginia after all the pain that I've caused and been through? Surely this was the best that I could have. When I woke up that morning, I had a strong desire burning in my soul to move forward and do something. I got up and I left. I went to the local hospital. I told them that I was going through addiction issues and I wanted some help. They kept me in there for about 3 days and a Social Worker suggested a place called the Ebony House. I didn't know anything about it, but they had an opening and I decided to go. It was in the East End of Phoenix, but I really didn't care, because by this time, I have been to multiple hospitals, different halfway houses, and various programs. I only stayed a couple of days in each one. I just didn't have any peace. I was like a Rolling Stone. I'm here one day and I'm gone tomorrow. I lived my whole life like that. I wasted so many days, and so many years, but the Ebony House kept me around for a while. It was an African American house of recovery, but they didn’t just take blacks, they accepted everyone. They had Islamic and Christian workers there.

It was not a religious program, but it was based on love and trying to help a person get out of their own way. I immediately embraced the concept of what they were trying to do. Each individual had to go through a process called *the Circle.* After being there for about 60 days and after you have completed certain aspects of the program, it was your turn for *the Circle. The Circle* consists of you sitting in the middle of the room with the Case Managers and your peers surrounding you. The first phase of *the Circle* consists of everybody telling you something negative about yourself based on the story of your life. You had to write your story and you had to read it in front of everybody during *the Circle.* So, after they heard your story, they would take notes and then respond to you about the negative things that you have done. All the negative things that they see about you. There were no holds barred and they were allowed to say anything to you they thought was negative.

You were told how bad of a father you were, and that you weren't shit as a man. You are a lazy motherfucker and that you need to get your shit together. You had to sit there and listen and not say a word. After everyone finishes, they would take the time to tell you the things that they saw that were positive in your life; all to build you up. It was a very life-changing experience, to sit there and take it. All that negative stuff, especially from people who are selfish like us alcoholics and addicts. For us to sit there and let people bombard us with all those negative thoughts about what they thought about you was a hard pill to swallow. It was good to hear people building you up. I wasn't any different when it was my turn. They let me have it too. They told me about myself and at the end, it gave me a lot of courage. It was time for me to make a decision about my life when I leave this program. I have been in contact with my wife and she was excited to have me come home. So, when I finished the first part of the program, I felt that I was good enough to leave. So, I asked my wife to send me a bus ticket. She sent me the bus ticket a few days later. I was excited about the opportunity to go home again. I lied and said that I was going home in two days to my wife, but I left the program the next day so that I would have at least 24hours left in the city to say goodbye to some of the people that I would miss. In all actuality, all I wanted to do was have 24 hours left to get high, and party a little bit before I head back to Virginia. See, all of that good stuff that I learned and all of that good stuff that I talked about in the program went out of the window, because it was all about me and what I wanted to do. So, I graduated the program and went out the door. I got the people from the program to drop me off at the Greyhound Station. I left the Greyhound and went back to 24th Street and Van Buren streets. I hung out that whole night. I got high and hung out with Ramos and Irma. I had a few people who tried to steal from me, but I just kept cool, because I knew I was leaving in the morning. The next morning, when it was time for me to leave, I had second thoughts. I didn't want to leave. Ramos went outside to get his bike and told me to ride with him to the Greyhound Bus Station and told me leave, because if I didn't somebody was going to kill me. I looked at him and he wasn't joking. He cared enough about me to make sure that I left, so I got back on the Greyhound and I headed back to Richmond, Virginia. I was done with Arizona, but Arizona wasn't done with me. I really didn't look forward to coming back home, because I really didn't see anything that was going to change. I already set myself up for failure, because as soon as I got out of the program, I started getting high again. I lied to my wife and I lied to the people in the program that I was going home, but nevertheless, I was headed to Richmond, Virginia. When I got there, things felt calm enough. It seemed like I was missed by my wife and my stepson. They tried to show me love so many times and I mean we really tried to make it work. We were still trying to hang on to this marriage. I wasn't ready to put in the work in that was needed, and I just felt like so many things were closing in on me at my home. We had a one-bedroom apartment with three people living in it. Sometimes we had six or seven people living in the house and I always felt like I had to go outside of the house to have peace. That wasn't always the case, but that's what I had told myself. I felt like I didn't have any respect in my home, and my wife was always in the middle. She wanted me to have peace, and she wanted her son to have peace. The two most important men in her life we're always at odds with each other and that's not because we hated each other, it was because I was just so very selfish and self-centered.

I did not allow myself to heal. I didn't know how to communicate, because I was so caught up in what I needed. We all have our issues, but I'm only going to focus on mine right now. So regardless of all the troubles that I had in my marriage, one thing I do know is that I contributed to the destruction of it greatly. I would make some efforts to improve myself and the situation in my home. I would go out and try to find a job for a week or two, but eventually, I'd end up back on the corner again. Why couldn't I shake this disease? Why must I continue to go back to corners and hanging out with crack pipes and bottles? I have such a desire to do better, and so many people wanted me to do better. So many people have prayed for me, from family members to clergy, but nevertheless, I found myself on the streets again ripping and running until one day, I was in a car with a group of guys. We all got pulled over and they ran IDs. They gave the IDs back to everyone else and told them that they could leave. I was asked, have I ever been to Arizona?

I said, "Yes sir, I just left there a few months ago."

They said, "Well sir, it looks like you might have to go back. You have an indictment for your arrest."

My mouth dropped, and I could not think of or imagine anything that Arizona would want me to come back for. Yes, I was a crackhead, an alcoholic, and homeless, but I don't recall doing anything that would warrant such a response. That was at least my thinking, anyway. So, they took me to jail in Richmond City. The United States Marshals had 72 hours to pick me up and if they didn't get there on time, I would be free to go. So, on the last day they showed up at the Richmond City Jail. They shackled me up and put me back on the plane to Arizona. It was so humiliating to ride on that airplane with two Marshals beside you; handcuffed, while having a coat draped over your arms. I felt the stares from all the people. They looked at me as if I was one of the most dangerous men in society, but I was just a little ole crack head from Virginia.

So, I arrived at Maricopa County Jail in Phoenix, Arizona. This is where I was starting the process of trying to figure out where I would spend my time in prison, or would I go back to Virginia as a free man. After being processed, I was in shock to find out what I was being charged for. I was being charged with distribution. When I received all my paperwork I was ushered upstairs to the pod where I would be living. As soon as I walked in all eyes were on me. In most prison or jail settings, you got to check out the new guy, but something strange happened on this particular day. All of the black guys walked over to me. They grabbed my mattress and all of my belongings and immediately made up my bed up and began telling me the ropes of the prison. See, the Arizona jail system was designed to help you to learn how to deal with the prison system. It was all based-on race. Blacks were only allowed to deal with blacks, eat with blacks, and you should never sit on any other races beds. Those were just a few of the rules and there were many. They also had people who they call Heads. These were the people who are responsible for their race. We would have to take orders and directions from the Heads, and you could not do anything that they didn't want you to do. This is all very new to me and it felt like I was going back to the 60's. Let's not forget that I'm from Richmond, Virginia, the capital of the confederacy, but this was on a level that I wasn't prepared for. I didn't know how to get out of this situation, so I resorted back to that which was comfortable to me, exercise, and the Bible. After a few weeks of being there, the people started to get to know me and I started to get more comfortable with everyone. People started to respect me as some type of leader, because I didn't speak like everybody else on the West Coast. I always had this type of Martin Luther, and Malcolm X mentality that I carried it with me when I spoke. We had a little recreation area that I was able to use to do Bible studies once a night for about 30 minutes to an hour. The guys could just come in and share testimonies, sing and I would give a little message of hope. We would go on about our business and no one had any problems with that. I had multiple races listening to me. I shared a lot about my past with many people in this prison. I noticed that sharing has always been a great tool for me to help others. People receive you more when you are open and honest about who you are and what you been through. People can relate and are more willing to listen. I use my pain as a way to help others, and it has become my greatest gift. The year was 2006, and something very important was about to happen.

It might not have been that important for other people, but for me it was big. You see, the Super Bowl was going to be played on January 2007, and Prince was going to be performing on the halftime show. You should already know by now that Prince, to me, was the greatest artist that ever lived. It was Prince's music that helped me get through a lot of difficult times as a young child. It was Prince's music that helped me get through a lot of difficult times on the streets and in prison, and he was the halftime act at the Super Bowl. There was also a historical significance to the game. There was an African American coach for the Indianapolis Colts, and an African American coach for the Chicago Bears. So, whoever won the game was going to make history. Maricopa County Jail always took the TV for any reason, but we hoped that we had the TV for the big game. We haven't had our TV in about a week when the Super Bowl came on. There was no evidence that we were going to get it, especially after all the crying we did. We were all upset, and we tried to petition and ask certain Deputies if we could watch the Super Bowl, but to no avail. The TV was pitch black and we couldn't see the Super Bowl, so I decided to go ahead and have a Bible study session. So, we all gathered into the rec area and started to sing and share testimonies. We had a beautiful ceremony and 15 minutes into my speech, one of the gentlemen who was sitting outside in the day area, ran into the rec area, and simply yelled out, "Duke Prince on!" My mouth dropped to learn that they allowed the Super Bowl to come on and secondly, Prince was on. So, what was I to do? I'm the biggest Prince fan on the planet. Was I going to shut down the Bible study or was I going to run out and leave everybody else? I had to think on it, because once again, I'm selfish. I don't want people to think badly about me, so I had to make a decision that would be best for me at that time. The Lord knows that I wanted to see Prince. Over the years I've waited and waited to see him get the kind of respect that he deserved. He was the baddest man on the planet, and everybody needed to know it. Most people didn't know or didn't want to admit it, but he was and still is. So, I stayed in the rec area, and I continue with the Bible study. After it was over, I went out to enjoy the rest of the game, but I had missed Prince, one of my childhood Idols.

He was just performing at the halftime Super Bowl and I missed it. At least I can say I that I missed it for God. So, after the Super Bowl was over, it was time to get back to the task of finding out whether I was going to prison or going back to Virginia. I still could not figure out how these people got my information when I had moved back to Virginia. I don't remember getting into any trouble with any Police Officers. I didn't get locked up at any time while I was in Arizona so how did they get my information to put an indictment on me in the first place? My lawyer read to me a statement from one of the Detectives. Then he explained to me how they got my information. As the Officer was trying to close out the case, he was trying to figure out who this guy named Duke was. Evidently, I was a part of an ongoing investigation. So, as he asked about it, one of the other Detectives in his office pulled up my name and my picture popped up.

He said, "Is this him?"

The Detective said, "Yes, that's him!"

So that's how they got the information to put out an indictment on me. I also remembered how this Undercover Cop got me involved. One day when I was hanging out on Vanburen Street, he and this other white officer came over to get some drugs from me. Now, I should have known better, and I should have been more cautious. It was two white men, who looked fairly healthy, and clean cut, driving a pickup truck. They wanted to buy some crack. I felt a little something in my soul, but my desire for crack and money won the battle of intelligences that day. So according to the statement, they came up and asked me for crack. I told him that I could get them some and I made a phone call. While I made the call, I was waiting for the guy to come, but the guy who was standing with me had a conversation with me about why I was out here.

He asked me, "Do I think that I could do better?"

He told me that there are other things that I could be doing besides this. I didn't understand why this man was asking me all of these questions and telling me these things. He wanted to buy drugs and his partner didn't park.

He just rode around in circles waiting for the transaction to take place. I see it all so clearly now, but at the time drugs and alcohol were more important to me. So, the boy came to the spot and gave me some drugs. I took a little piece off the top and put it in my pocket, then I gave the rest to the cop.

The Undercover Cop said, “Man that's mighty small!”

I said, “That's all he got man. That's a 40! I can't do nothing else for you.”

So, he took it and they both got in the car and left. I grabbed the little pieces that he gave me, and I went over to my spot that I had in the abandoned wooded area. I would always go there to get high and get out of the heat. That's why they couldn't find me after the transaction was over, because they were too busy looking to see who was in the car. I don't know what happened to the guy in the car, but I never saw him again. All I can say is that I hope he didn't get into any serious issues because of my transgressions. So, it appears that they are charging me with distribution, or perhaps they're trying to get me to snitch on someone or provide more information, but there's nothing more to tell them. I was just a crackhead wanting crack. I was just trying to get high and get a drink. I don't have anything else to tell them. I really didn't know the guy’s name, and many months had passed since I was brought here in this jail cell. So, after all was said and done, they finally went down to a three-year plea bargain. I was still kind of upset about that, but I prayed over it weeks before my trial and suddenly, a great peace came upon me and I decided to take it. So, I was sentenced to three and a half years in the Arizona Department of Corrections. I was about to be sent to one of the most dangerous prison systems in the country, but in all actuality, I was just going to prison again.

I finally got shipped out of the jail to prison. My mind was really wondering about this great segregated system that I am about to enter. After a few weeks at one of Arizona's receiving facilities, I was transferred to my first stop, a place called Fort Grant. It was an old army base transformed into a prison. It was beat down, but it was also huge.

After my arrival, one of the officers guided me to my new living quarters. I was looking to see if any beds were available, and to my amazement, the officer didn't assign me to any of the beds that were empty. There were five beds empty and he called the command station and said he couldn't find any beds for the new inmate. I looked at him in bewilderment, because we just walked past a few beds.

I simply asked, "Excuse me officer, what's wrong with any of these beds?"

He said," You can't have any of those beds!"

I said, "Why not?"

He said, "Because they're not black beds."

Now me, being the smart-ass that I was, I looked at all the beds and they were painted gray. There was not one black, white, or green bed. All of them were painted gray so when he told me that there weren't any black beds, I simply said, "We'll can I have a gray one?"

I swear, if I could have read his mind, I believe he would have said, "Stop being such a smart ass nigger," but in all actuality, what he was trying to say was that all the beds were assigned to certain races. The beds that were open were assigned to other races. They didn't have any beds available for me so they had to make some arrangements to move some other people around so that I can have a black bed. My bed was right by the door. That's where they put everybody who just arrives. It was one of the most uncomfortable places I could be right by that door. There was so much trash and noise all night long. There were so many rules I had to learn, and this was a serious place. I saw Skinheads, Aryan Nation dudes, MS-13 dudes, and the Nation of Islam dudes. I said to myself, what the hell am I doing here? I'm just a crack head from Virginia who got caught up and now I'm in one the most dangerous prison systems in the country. I, being the chameleon that I am, was able to adjust. I started to work out and find church. Those were my main things, and my comfort zones. They also had a band room and each day; a race would have the opportunity to spend time there. I love all kinds of music and the band room was always situated right in front of the

Chow Hall. So, when we are in line waiting for chow, we could hear the various bands playing. There was a country band, a rock band, a R&B band, a top 40 band and all of them were top-notch. I saw some of the baddest musicians I've ever met in my life in Fort Grant. Occasionally, I would go in and talk to the guys in the black band. There was this guy named Duck and he was one of the baddest musicians I ever met. He could play everything. He could sing, write and he was the best musician on the camp. He also happened to be a black guy. He wanted me to come and join the band, but I had hesitations at first because, I didn't want to commit to anything, and I don't always get along with others, because I was selfish and self-centered. I wanted things to go my way, but I kept coming because I loved music. I eventually joined the band, and I had no doubt that we could have been big if we were out on the street. Each person in the group was able to get off on one instrument and go to the next one. Each member could also sing. I didn't realize that I could sing and play the drums at the same time until I actually tried. We would play Purple Rain, Stevie Wonder, Earth Wind & Fire, Pieces of a Dream and much more. We were bad and everybody knew it. Duck was the keyboard player, and the best drummer I've ever seen. He showed me some things on the drums that I never thought was possible. I practiced, but I just couldn't get some of those rudiments. That brother stayed in the band room. That was his life. He was so good that even some of the white bands allowed him to come and play the drums and nobody said anything. There was a local Bible study that took place outside. All the races were allowed to go to it, and no one had any issues. I would go on Saturdays and Sundays. I would go to the church, but the church was very political, and it was run by the Whites. The whites controlled it. They talked about love, forgiveness, and happiness, but it was very political. The one held on the yard was more free. It was more open, and the people felt more comfortable. I went to that one most of the time. Once in a while I would have the opportunity to share my thoughts and views. Soon after, they started asking me to share a message and I would. As usual, I was well-received, because of the manner in which I would do it. I would always use my personal pain to teach spiritual principles. People can always relate to pain.

I wish more people would use their pain in their efforts to help someone else. So, after a few months of this routine the gentleman who ran the outside bible study all of a sudden quit and gave up. I didn't know why he did it, and I tried to talk to him multiple times, because I really didn't want to take on this task. This was a whole different world, and I didn't know how people were going to receive me in this racial environment, trying to lead a bunch of men in peace, harmony, and togetherness. This was an environment that produced separation and division. I didn't want any part of it, but I couldn't help it. It was like I had to do it. The brother invited me over to his living quarters and told me that he was about to go home, and he felt that God wanted me to take over that fellowship. He gave me a Bible that I still have to this day. It was a study edition of the Open Bible Study Bible. It is torn and raggedy, but I adore it. I became the Worship Leader again in this prison. The job that I had at the prison was a Tutor. I had a pretty good job and it wasn't hard. I didn't have to go out into the elements and that was a nice. I assisted the prisoners to get GED's and this is was my life at Fort Grant. I would always catch flak from a lot of the guys in the band because they wanted me to spend more time with them, but I had to spend more time at the Fellowship. Once again, I had to choose in the summer of 2007. A riot was about to break out and everybody was going around sharing information. All races had meetings in the Open Fields. One of the biggest challenges that blacks had was that we always had to figure out who we were going to side with, even if it was none of our business. If a fight breaks out, you have to choose a side. I hated those who had the right to tell me that I had to choose a side, but that was the reality that I was living in. If the whites had a problem with the Mexicans, we had to choose who we were going to side with. In most cases, it would be the Mexicans because, the whites didn't want to have anything to do with blacks, but the Mexicans would side with the whites if they were against us. Everybody was against us, so we always had to walk a fine line. I had a lot of respect on the yard and I was only there for a few months. It just seemed that people who walked in love didn't have any issues, especially if you were authentic.

That particular riot never broke out, but it scared me to death. What are you going to do in your own living quarters when I riot is breaking out on the field somewhere? You got Whites, Mexicans and Native Americans looking around deciding should they fight, or should they attack another race. It was totally and utterly based and rooted in ignorance. By the grace of God, I never got to experience such violence while I was in that prison system.

One evening, I was chilling out in my living quarters, I and was called to the Sergeant's office. I know didn't get into any trouble so why would I need to go to her office. So, as I headed there, I notice that things where a little too quiet, but I kept it moving. When I met the Sargent, she asked me to sit down in her office. She was a hard no non-sense lady that no one liked. She smoked like a sailor and looked as hard as any man I have known. She asked me about my father, and I said to myself, oh lord, not now.

She said, "Mr. Dukes your father has died."

I just looked at her stunned, and asked her could I call my Aunt, and she agreed. What happened next would hurt me for years to come.

I called my Aunt Ruth and we talked briefly about what had happened. My father died in his sleep in Cradock. It is a small section in Portsmouth where my father lived by himself. My aunt said that she would be handling all of his affairs.

I said, "Well, I know I'm not going to be able to come Aunt Ruth, but you can tell everyone I said hello and why I can't be there."

She said, "I won't tell them where you are."

I said, "I don't care what they know Aunt Ruth."

Then she let me have it. She says, "Well Tubby, I don't want to tell nobody, because I'm ashamed of you. Look how old you are. You don't have a car, a house, a job, or nothing. You are just wasting your life away and your mother would be so ashamed."

That was the blow that hurt, and I couldn't say anything. So, I took it and I said my goodbyes. As I walked back to my living area, I felt nothing. I hated my father, but I didn't know how to handle the grief, so I just put it away and focused on my time here at Fort Grant. Now my father and mother where both gone, and I was all alone. I did have a wife and a son, but it didn't look like it. There was no healing for me, but I pressed on. Well, my time at Fort Grant was getting to be a little monotonous. I was doing the same things over and over again, and I was getting consumed with people pulling me in different directions. The band wanted me to do this, the church wanted me to do that, and the Fellowship on the yard wanted me to do something else. My job had its own expectations, but I didn't know what I wanted to do. All I knew was that I was tired of Fort Grant. I put in numerous requests to be transferred to another facility. I had done a good job there and I didn't get into any trouble so, I really wanted to move. I finally got approved to move to another facility. It was a low-risk facility. It was a brand-new facility and the people who went there were in the process of going home. I might of have had a year or so left at that particular time. It was around the summer of 2008. I was able to obtain a Tutors position. It kept me off the radar and it kept me from doing other hard and tedious tasks, but the racism factor was still there. The racism wasn't as prominent at this facility, because the people were trying to go home. It was time to leave the politics aside as we were transitioning back into society. Nevertheless, you still had to eat with your race, and you couldn't sit on other races beds. Time went on as usual and wouldn't you know it, I became the leader of the church there. Multiple races would come to the Fellowship, and I had a lot of respect from the race heads at that unit, but there was a storm brewing that no one expected in 2008. There was heated political conversations all around the country dealing with Hillary Clinton and Barack Obama. The possibility of a black president was looming ever so closely. I was conflicted about the idea because I liked the Clintons and I thought Hillary was the best candidate and the most qualified candidate to ever run for office. I educated myself on all the political issues. I watched Fox, CNN, and I learned a lot about caucuses and primaries. I had political discussions with people from different races. There's one thing about me that a lot of people don't know. If there's something that I do not know I would take the time out to learn about it, even if I'm uncomfortable with it, or don't agree with it, just so I can have a conversation about it. I think it's very important for men to be able to have a conversation on many levels, sports, politics, religion, history, and economics. It is important for us to be informed, but it's another thing for us to apply that which we know. That has always been my issue. I can have a whole world of knowledge in my head and end up sleeping under a bridge with a crack pipe in my mouth, but that was me. I was a sponge soaking up everything. As the election loomed closer, I could hear certain conversations from the Skinheads and the Aryan Nation guys talking about assassination attempts and how they were going to do it, and when it would take place if Barack Obama would win. Besides, this would never happen here in America, but Barack Obama did win the Democratic Nomination. It was huge and the possibility became much closer. Barack only had to beat John McCain which was no small order, because McCain was a Senator and a war hero. To tell you the truth, I had a lot of respect for John McCain, because he said what he felt, and he believed in what he said. I respected that about him, but I wanted Barack Obama to win. I would tell a person in a heartbeat don't vote for a person based on her or his race, gender, or political affiliation. Vote for the person whose ideas stand closest to your values and the things that you hold dear, but in 2008, I wanted the brother. I wanted the black man to be President. Now, I educated myself on his policy and he was a good talker. He had a lot of great ideas, but this is going to be a challenge because many people didn't want him to be President just because he was black. Just as many people wanted him to be President just because he was black. If he won the office, he would already come in with a load on his shoulders that previous presidents did not have to carry. So, after Fall draws near, the election rhetoric became more heated and the debates became more entertaining. Election night is finally here. After getting off my job, I quickly ate, and I was ready for Election Night. It was just like watching a football game. I had to get myself together and make sure all things are in place so that I could see the final results. I had to get up early so I couldn't stay up to see all the results so, I laid down around 9:10 p.m. I then heard a black guy run through the facility screaming, "Obama, Obama, Obama!"

I just laid in my bed and cried. What had just happened? There was a black President! I can still feel the tears rolling down my eyes. I still can feel the pride bursting out of my soul and I also can still feel the hatred amongst those around me. The next morning you could hear a pin drop. After all, we were in Arizona, one of the most racist prisons in America and the white racist nationalist inmates were loud, bold, and angry. They dared us to say anything. They dared us to respond to the hatred and the evil rhetoric that they spewed on a daily basis. We endured many, many, more painful expressions, and it didn't just come from the whites, but from the Mexicans as well. At least the Mexicans could understand the plight of the black man because they were the niggers of the West Coast, nevertheless, as time went on, people became more comfortable with their reality. Either you loved Obama, or you hated him. So, as 2009 ushered in, there's a lot of pride in my heart, because I knew that this was my year to go home. I am about to leave Arizona. I made it through, and I still had about six or seven months left, but I was blessed. I was in a good spot, and I was doing well. I was just as healthy and muscular as I ever been. I was also as spiritually fit as I ever been. I am ready to go home and become a productive member of society. One of the Counselors came to me with a bright idea. They wanted to do a one-week session on cultural diversity. She came to me because one of the teachers told her that I liked to teach and that I was good it. So, she pulled me into the office and told me about a new class. The Department of Corrections wanted to Institute this class, because of the high racial divide in the prison. They wanted to promote cultural diversity and bring different races together and have a conversation about how they think. She wanted me to teach it. I felt very proud to be chosen for this task, but I also knew that it was going to be an issue, because it was not the church service that people can come and leave all the politics outside. This wasn't a church service; it's a mandatory institutional class. The people that wouldn't normally come to church would be in this class as well. How would the Aryan Nations, and the Mexicans deal with having a black guy teaching this class on cultural diversity. Nevertheless, I decided to accept it, because it was a challenge. It was something that I never done, and it was something that I could add to my resume. So, I took on that challenge and the very first class that we had, there were like five skinheads in the class.

They made it known that they didn't want to be there, and the teacher was in there for the first class. We all took roll and she explained what would take place for the first week. She introduced me and then walked out. There I was, face-to-face with many people in the room hating me just because of the way I looked. So, I was called to share cultural diversity. We had our conversations, discussions, and questions.

One day, one of the skinheads said, “We got too much stuff going on in our country to worry about trying to be diverse.”

I allow him to share his feelings and after he finished, I simply asked him,” So what do you think is the source of all these problems? If we can get to the root of these problems, then maybe we can deal with them.”

He said, “It was the Jews.”

He had a cross around his neck, and I asked, “Are you a Christian?”

He said, “Yes!”

I said, “So am I. Do you believe in Jesus?”

He said, “Yes!”

I said, “So do I. Did you know Jesus was a Jew?”

He said, “Absolutely not, that was something that they set up so that the Jews can have power in the world.”

Soon after many other people raised their hands and gave answers. It appeared that many of them had ideas and thoughts on Jesus and many of them consider themselves to be Christians even though they didn't attend the church services. It was an awesome discussion and it all went back to one thing. Since we were talking about Jesus, what was the nature of Jesus? Everybody agreed that he walked in love. So, if we agree that Jesus walked in love and we all say that we believe in Jesus and that we all follow Jesus; then wouldn't it be a good idea if we can implement that simple tool in our lives? It was being revealed to me that many of these men didn’t believe in those political, jail house rules, and ideologies until they came to prison and got with a click or group. In Arizona it was made by force.

When it was all said and done, teaching this class showed me a lot about myself. I was capable of great things. I was very proud of how the classes went and I earned a lot of respect from the whole yard that day. I wish I had that same respect at home. I was about to go home, and I had been in constant contact with my wife. I wanted to share something with her, because I wanted to have a fresh start when I came home. I decided to tell her about the affair I had with the nurse at the nursing home in a letter. She said that she already knew about it, but when she read the words from me, it caused a great pain in her that I don't believe ever healed. Those three years in Arizona really changed some things in our marriage. I didn't want to believe, it but it was. I wasn't home the whole time we were married. I was either on the streets or in prison. When I was clean, it was for a brief period of false hope. I imposed my will on people who cared about me. I only cared about my own self-interest. My wife told me that she had got sick and I didn't know to what degree, but I was still willing to make my marriage work. She also told me that she was in the house alone. I had always had issues with living in the house with too many people. We only had a one-bedroom apartment and there were times that many people were in the house. Even with my stepson there, it was just too crowded. I felt like my peace was being compromised. We talked about it and she assured me that the house would be empty, but it was more about my selfishness than anything else. When it was time for me to come home, I was scared. I was about to leave an environment that had given me many things, hope, respect courage, education, skills, and drive. All that came from prison. I was very nervous as I took the flight back to Virginia. It gave me time to contemplate what was before me. What would I do differently? Would I destroy everything again?

I really wanted to change, and so many people were pulling for me. I had been given some of the best tools one could ever have, freedom, hope, and opportunity. When I arrived in Richmond, no one was there to greet me, so I had to catch a cab back to my home. Being in Richmond was bittersweet, because it meant that I was home. It reminded me that I had much work to do. I had a lot of pain to deal with, but was I ready? We'll see. To my surprise, when I arrived home and knocked on the door, my stepson opened it and he greeted me with open arms. I thought he was just visiting. By the way, the front room looked, he was living there. When I saw my wife, she was smiling so hard. She was so glad to see me, but I notice that something wasn't right. She was a little slower than normal and had a little shaking to her. She pulled me in the room and told me that my stepson had broken up with his girlfriend and that is why he was here. Now, I just had this conversation with her a day ago, and she told me that no one was there. I think she might have thought that if she tells me the truth about the living conditions, and the severity of her illness, that I wouldn't had come home. Now, I might have thought about other living arrangements, because history dictates that I wouldn't do well in this environment, not because she was sick. I figured it's all on me if I do well or not. Regardless of the circumstances, I can choose to live or die.

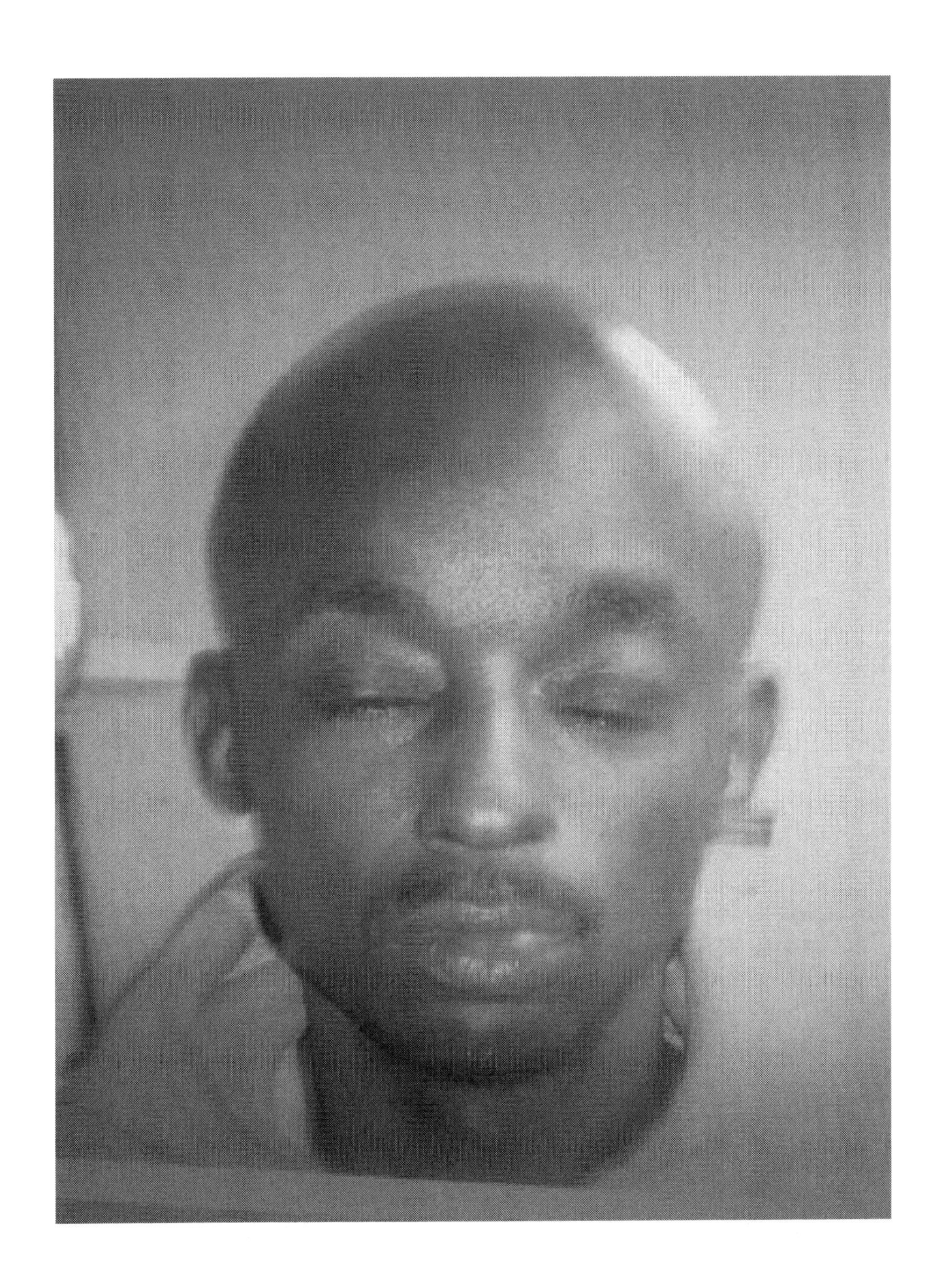

# JUST NOT READY

I needed to contact my aunt and my son. Eventually I did and the healing process began. I was really making some progress. I was earning money doing day labor work, and I was going to church. The things in the house wouldn't change me over night, but I was praying that God would notice my efforts and bring peace between my stepson and I, but for some strange reason we just could not get on the same page. He was going through his own demons and issues. There was also a wife and a mother who was stuck in the middle of this. She wasn't in the best of health. All she wanted was for us to try to get along. Things didn't go my way in the house like I thought, and I felt they should. I couldn't deal with the stress of the house, so once again I would try to find peace in the streets. A sense of peace that came outside on the corners, and in front of stores drinking with the fellas. In my mind, once again, I would say, if I could just drink, everything will be okay. That was how I dealt with life. I'd run away from my issues and problems. There was a guy named Travis who loaned me some money to help me get back on my feet. He was the son of the gentleman who owned the company that I used to work for called Chesapeake Bay Cabinet Company. Travis always wanted to see me do well. He got together with some of his church friends and they gave me about $400. I gave some money to my wife and my stepson. I went out with good intentions, but I ended up smoking crack. I stayed out for four days and what happened next will change the course of my marriage. After being out for those days, I finally came home, and my wife was already mad at me and I found out that she had called my friend Travis. She told him that I had spent all the money that he gave me. She also told him that she needed some money for the light bill, and he gave it to her. I had no reason to be upset because of what I did, and I knew that I spent all the money up, but however, I was angry because she had told our private business to someone. It really bothered me when someone would tell my personal business, but she had a right to be angry. Once again, I had done the same thing. I got back on drugs and stayed on the streets. I had become an irresponsible, lying, and cheating dog. I regressed back to the same individual that I was before.

So, I'm standing in the house with her looking like death and I have the nerve to be upset, because she told my business while I was gone for four days. So, we argued about it and we argued about it. Then her son came home and heard us arguing. He came in the room and asked why I was arguing with his mother? Then he hit me, and we tousled for a moment and he walked away and said that I needed to leave. I looked at my wife and she didn't say a word. I was standing there in bewilderment, because her son had just assaulted me, and she didn't say anything. At that moment, I knew things would never be the same again. I felt my marriage was over and I take 99.9% of all the blame. So, I left, and the streets were going to be my home. I found myself in abandoned houses, and underneath bridges. I found myself doing a couple of stints in jail. A month here and a couple of days there and then I started to go back and forth to the different hospitals. I learned that I could call an ambulance and tell them that I was suicidal, they would take me to one of the facilities. They would keep me for a few days. That gave me an opportunity to get some rest and get some food. That is how I survived for a few months. On one occasion, at one of the hospitals, my wife talked to one of the Counselors. We were trying to figure out if we could work out our marriage. As soon as we talked about the assault that happened, things went south. She was so worried that I was going to call the Police on him.

She said, "If you called the Police then she's going to tell them what she saw."

I was in awe at what I just heard. What else could you have seen other than your son hitting me. Yes, we were hollering, and screaming at each other, but I have never ever put my hands on any woman; based on the life that I lived as a child. I saw my father abuse my mother. I've done many things in my life that were disrespectful and dishonorable, but I have never to this day, ever put my hands on a woman. I'm not proud of many things that I've done, but I am proud of that. I just left it alone. I wasn't going to press charges anyway, because I felt so guilty about the way that I lived, so I just stayed away, living on the streets of Richmond. I found myself living in one woman's house or another.

I stayed under bridges, in cars, or on corners with no direction or life purpose. How did my life take this turn again, how? Can a man with so much talent and so much to give, be eating out of trash cans, sleeping under bridges, hang on corners with bums, alcoholics, crackheads, and prostitutes? I was the worst of them. I looked like walking death. I was 130 pounds, skinny, black, and destitute with no hope, and purpose in life. I was just existing walking the streets. There is no way that I could come back from this one. There isn't anyone that loves me anymore. I have burned every bridge possible. Thanksgiving was approaching and I used to always gather with the guys in front of Lowe's on Broad Street. This is where we would meet up and drink, talk, panhandle, and steal whatever we could to get through the rest of the day. On Thanksgiving morning, we decided that we were going to go to the Convention Center to get something to eat. It was around 7 or 8 in the morning. I was already exhausted from drinking that morning, so I decided to go to my little spot and take a nap. I went to the Lee Bridge, crawled underneath and took a nap. It was just me, the bottles, and the crack pipes. The smell of urine and feces surrounded me. I went to sleep, but to my surprise it was pitch black when I woke up. I had no idea what time it was, so I grabbed my bag, hopped the fence, and went across the street to the local 7-Eleven. I found out that it was about 8 at night, so I decided to reach in my bag and grab my pack of noodles. I made a soup with all the fixings, and then took it back to the bridge. I sat there and ate my Thanksgiving dinner. I ate in the darkness with my friends, guilt, shame, and pain. As I looked around, I didn't see a squirrel moving or a bird chirping. How did I get here? How did I find myself in this position again? Is this all that I have to offer? Why am I even here on this earth? Something has to be better than this. So, I woke up the next morning, and I headed back towards Broad Street to greet all of my friends. I just looked at them and I kept walking. I didn't want to have anything to do with them, but it didn't stop me from getting high or drinking in other places. I eventually went back to the fellas, but a change would soon come. This change happened on the campus of VCU in 2011.

September can be a crazy month. Summer is leaving, winter is trying to come in and fall does not know what it wants to do. You can have 90-degree days and 30-degree nights which was normally the case in 2011. On one of those September days, I was hanging out with the guys on Broad Street. I found myself having been on a good 3 to 4 months run, on the streets. I barely ate and I was just surviving. I was just drinking and trying to get high. On a particular evening I was with this white guy named Monk. He was really cool with everybody. We were close. We would go panhandle and drink together. One day we found ourselves walking the streets of the VCU Campus. It was around 8 in the evening and we saw this white guy staggering towards us. He asked us if we wanted something to drink and we said yes. He invited us to his house on the campus since it was getting cool outside. It was supposed to be in the thirties that night. We really appreciated the opportunity, and we went to his house and made ourselves comfortable. Now many of you might not know anything about Richmond or VCU. If you have lived on the streets of Richmond, you know not to fuck around on the VCU Campus or you're going to jail. Nevertheless, we found ourselves inside his home. He said we could spend the night so we could get off the street and we thought we had hit the jackpot. He was willing to buy us cigarettes and beer and let us spend the night. What more could you ask for. Then he happened to ask a question that changed everything. I believe he asked the question that changed my life.

He said, "Do you guys know where I can get some crack from?"

My eyes lit up, because of course I knew where the crack was at and it wasn't that far away; maybe three or four blocks at the most. So, he asked my friend and I if we would go get some crack and some more beer. So he gave us a $50 bill and we thought that we were in heaven. We decided that we would go get the stuff, but there was a thought in the back of my mind to not come back with the money. What sense would that make to take $50 from someone who's trying to buy drugs, beer and cigarettes for you and is going to allow you to stay in his house.

It just didn't seem like a bright idea at the time, so we went to find the crack, but the crack house was closed. No one was around and it was too cold to go find something else. We went to the store and bought beer, wine and cigarettes and went back to his house. As we approached the house, I was able to see that the door was cracked. It was about 6 inches open. Now we knew that we had left that door open, but nevertheless, we walked up and pushed the door open. We walked into a house that was totally silent. We called the gentleman's name over and over, but we didn't want to be too loud, because we didn't want to startle any of the neighbors. We didn't see anyone. There were cigarette butts still in the ashtrays and the bottles that we left on the tables prior to our exit, but we didn't see our host. So, we walked into a bedroom and he was there laying on his bed. We just looked at each other with bags of beer, wine, and the remaining cash in my pocket. You would had thought that we would have just sat there, drink and pass out, while enjoying the warmth of the house. Instead I happened to look at our host while he was sleeping and saw an envelope sticking out of his shirt. I pointed to it, and my friend grabbed it. He looked inside and pulled out about seven or eight hundred-dollar bills. We looked at each other not knowing what to do so he shrugged his shoulders as to say what's up. I shrugged my shoulders as to say what's up. So, he put the money in his pocket, and I grabbed the bags of beer and we left on. Now this is around 11 p.m. We were on the cold streets, but we had a pocketful of money, beer, and cigarettes. We could have easily gone and got a room, but we didn't see the need of paying for a room for only a few hours. We knew that we weren't going to sleep so we braved the cold for that night. We slept under the bridge and drunk all night trying to stay up so that we wouldn't freeze to death. We tried to make plans about what we were going to do the next day. We were going to get a room for a few days and party with alcohol, crack, women and weed. The next morning that's what we did. We tried to shake ourselves off and get a hotel room. We picked up a couple of cases of beer, some cigarettes, and invited a few girls. We got us some crack and had a good old time for about 2 or 3 days. When the crack was gone, we still had a few hundred dollars left.

For some strange reason we didn't buy any more crack. We just kept drinking and drinking. I don't remember eating that much at all. Four days after all the crack was gone, I remember waking up one morning to use the bathroom. I did my business, washed my hands, and looked in the mirror and for the first time in my life I did not recognize who was looking back at me. It was as if death was trying to show me that I would visiting him very soon. I just stared at myself. I could see the bone structures in my face. I could see my sunken cheekbones, and swollen eyes. I had this helpless look of despair on my face and I said to myself that I was done. I walked out to the room. We still had beer all over the place and we still had some money left over. I told him that I was gone. He asked me where I was going, and I told him that I'll be back in a little while. I left that room and I just walked. I didn't know where I was going, and I didn't have any money. I had burned every resource available to me. I definitely wasn't going back to my wife, especially in this condition. At this rate, I was going to end up either in prison, jail or dead if I didn't do something real soon. So, I stopped in my tracks and I asked someone if they would call 911 for me. An ambulance came and took me to one of the local hospitals where they checked me in. I knew I wasn't going to be able to stay for a long, because I have already burned these bridges, but I just needed a day or two. I just needed someone to talk to. I was able to talk to one of the Counselors and there were only a few options for me. One was to go to The Healing Place. It's a facility where I had already been multiple times and I just wasn't ready for that type of program again. It was a long-term treatment program and it was very strict. It was very serious, and it was very hard from my point of view. I got that from the two or three times I tried to complete the program. So, she gave me another option, The Salvation Army Rehabilitation Center. I decided that I would try that. So, on October 3rd, 2011, I checked into the Salvation Army Rehabilitation Center for men.

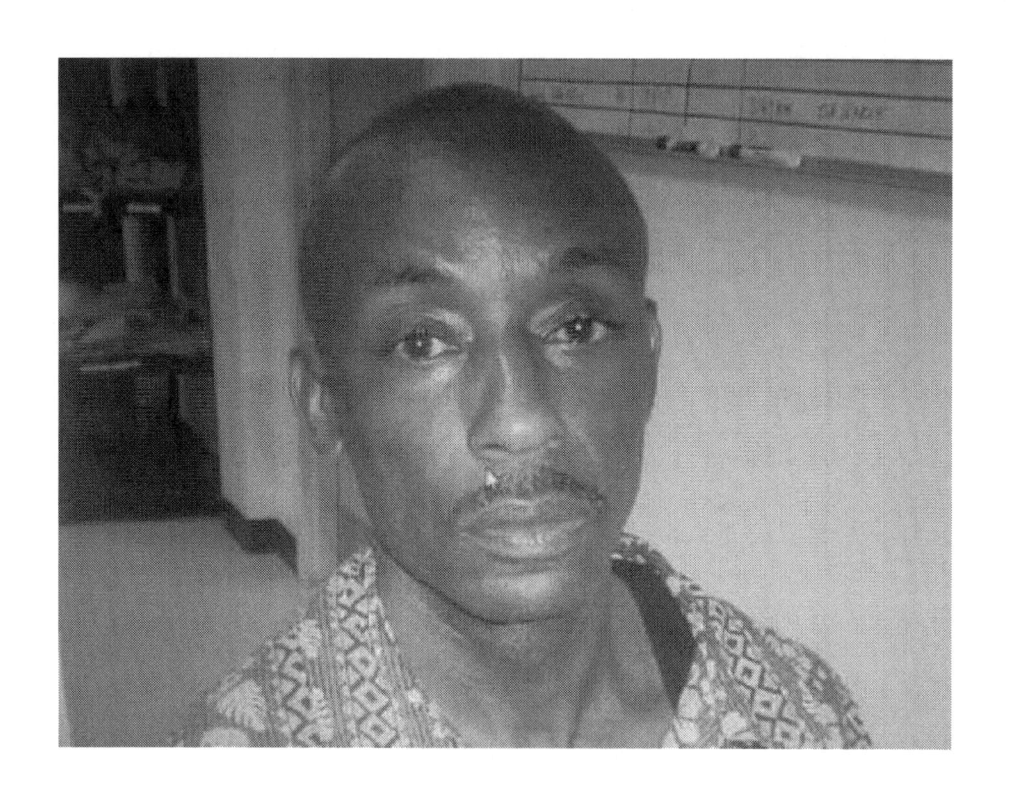

# THE SALVATION ARMY

I was in really bad shape. I was all about 130 pounds and I was still very weak. This was a Christian program and I didn't have any problem with that. To be honest, I did not go into the program, because I was ready to change my life completely and give it over to the Lord. I came into this program, because I was tired of sleeping on the streets and I needed some help with my court case. I was looking at some time with my previous record. I just knew I was going to jail, but if I could get some help through the program, the outcome could get better for me. To be honest, I wasn't holding my breath. At least I had a place to stay, I was warm, and I was off the streets. There was a married couple who ran the program. The husband was the Program Director, but in my opinion, his wife was the person in charge. I began working on one of the donation trucks as one of my duties. I worked with one of the employees from the Salvation Army and we would drive throughout the community to pick up donations and bring them back to the warehouse. At the end of the day, I would come in, take my shower, and prepare myself for dinner and any other programs that I might have to participate in as a part of my duties. The experiences that I had on the truck were horrific. It wasn't because of the job; it was because of the guy driving the truck. He had just graduated the program and he was blessed with a job, but all he wanted to do was go to this girl's house and sniff heroin. From time to time he would park somewhere, nodding off, but he would do this while we were driving while we on the highway. We always got back to the facility late. I was so tired, and I had to continue doing my programming. Plus, I was 130 pounds, trying to get my strength back. I was so weak and tired, and the last thing I needed to do was be associated with a dude that's getting high every day. So, I went to gentleman named Rocky. He was the Warehouse Manager at the time. I shared my feelings about what was going on. I didn't share information about the guy getting high, but I stated that I couldn't handle coming in late all the time. I have only been there a short time, less than a month and I was already complaining about not being able to do the work or my job, but these where legitimate complaints. So that morning, when it was time to go to work, Rocky pulled me in the office.

He asked me, "Do you think you can handle working at the auction?"

I said, "I would do anything that I need to do. I'm a good worker Rocky. Please do not allow my complaints or my stature dictate in your mind, who I am."

He said, "I need a man over there that I can trust and can do the work."

So, I received a new title and I was transferred to the auction facility. The Salvation Army Auction was a very unique place, it was a world within itself. When the items didn't sell in the store, they get loaded up on the auction truck and taken from the warehouse right across the street into the auction building. This is where I would take the items off the truck and set them up in the auction house. The auctions would be held on Wednesdays and Fridays. The Auctioneer was a gentleman named Patrick. He was also a graduate of the program. He was a real cool dude and we got along very well. The beauty of it all was that I had the opportunity to work by myself. I could cut the radio on, clean up and set up items as I saw fit. Now, one of my best gifts was my ability to connect with people. I became close with a lot of the customers. I brought a different atmosphere to the auction. The auction started to break records and the whole place was making more money than the auction has ever made. Honestly, I don't know if that was all because of me, but I would sure like to think that I had something to do with it. I know that my skills with setting up, and my personality with the men at the facility, and the customers; I was definitely a positive light to many. Things are going very well for me and I was thriving at the Salvation Army. Once again, I became a leader in this religious program. I started to share my thoughts and opinions on certain things. We also had a gentleman named Chaplin Isaiah. He was a young, black man whom I always enjoyed talking to and shared things with. Everything was really going well for me in the program. The Director and his wife grew very close to me. They even decided that they were going to help me in my court case. Communications were even developing between my wife and me. After all the pain and loss, we were communicating again.

Every night I would try to read my scriptures and after work, I would try to exercise. A routine was coming back in my life. Life was starting to show up. There was a poisonous lady in my life that I met when I was on the street. She wanted me to come and see her every week, but every time I got a pass, she would want me to come and spend the night with her. I did on a couple occasions, but the environment was toxic for me. I knew that I could not live like this if I was going to stay clean at the Salvation Army. She already had a few mental health issues and all she wanted to do was smoke weed. After she gets high, all she wanted to do was argue, fuss, and then have sex. I just could not function like that. I would go to Sunday services to hear the word of God; even though the messages came from different perspectives, different upbringings, and different ideologies, I was okay with it. Anything that I could use I would keep and anything I didn't agree with, I would store away to possibly use it for another time. I still had to deal with this court case, and by the Salvation Army only being a 6-month program, April 1st was my graduation date and the month of March was my big court case. One day before my court case, the Commonwealth Attorney called me, no not my Lawyer. The Commonwealth's Attorney called, and he asked me how I was doing and that he wanted to have a discussion with me about my case. So, I listened to him and I told him that I have been offered a job at the Salvation Army and how well I was doing in the program. So, the Commonwealth's Attorney asked me a question that I didn't think that any Commonwealth Attorney would ever be asking me.

He asked, "Do you think you might want to do probation?"

I had to pause for a moment, because I couldn't really believe what I was hearing.

"Are you trying to tell me that, with my record and background, that you are offering me probation?"

He said, "Yes, but it's not final. It's up to the judge, but that's what I would offer."

I said, "Yes sir, I would like that!"

He said, "Okay Mr. Dukes, we'll see you tomorrow."

I said, “Yes sir, thank you for calling!”

When I hung up the phone, I felt a sense of joy. I felt a sense of praise, relief, and change coming in my life. I wanted to scream. I was inside the auction house by myself, but I wanted to yell because the power of God was showing up in my life. I haven't felt this in a long time because of all the negative things that have been going on in my life. There was so much pain and loss, but things were looking and feeling different. The Commonwealth’s Attorney had offered me probation! I shared this with everyone, and I took the rest of the day off to prepare for my court case. The next morning, the Program Director and his wife drove me to court.

I must admit that I was a little nervous, and to say that I wasn’t would be a lie, but I also had a sense of great peace, because I knew that the Commonwealth's Attorney was suggesting that I get probation instead of jail time for my case. Remember that I am a black man who was going to court. I am a man who has been to jail, and prison multiple times in different states. There is no way that I should be able to receive probation or parole, but I trust you God and I went with it. For the first time I was at peace with knowing that if I did go to jail, this would be the first time that I will go to jail in the right state of mind. I was at peace with who I was. I was healthy and I wasn't on drugs or alcohol. So, if something happened, I was able to make peace with it, but it doesn't mean that I wanted to go to prison. The Program Director, his wife and I walked into the courtroom. I had a court appointed attorney, and I'm grateful for all that he tried to do, but all he really wanted to do was find a way to make a deal with the State that would be beneficial for himself. So, I really didn't know what to expect or what would transpire; all final decisions were left up to the Judge, but here we go. The Judge walks into the courtroom to the familiar phrase, “All rise!”

Everyone stands up and then we are seated. After a few simple arraignment cases go by I finally heard my name called. The State versus Clinton Dukes, Jr., and all parties. I stood up to approach the bench with my Lawyer and the Commonwealth and their attorney to the other side.

The Judge asked the Commonwealth Attorney, "Has an agreement been made?"

The Commonwealth Attorney said, "Yes!"

He gives a copy of the agreement to my Lawyer and takes a copy of the agreement up to the Judge with a folder of my personal history. It was silent in the courtroom as the Judge looked over the folder, moving his fingers up and down the documents in the file. He looked up at me and looked back at the records. He looks at the plea agreement and then looks back at me.

Then he said, "Mr. Dukes, will you please stand?"

He looks directly at me and holds up the plea agreement, and he says, "Mr. Dukes, do you know what this is?"

I said, "Yes you're Honor, its plea agreement."

He said, "Yes, it is Mr. Dukes, but it's also something else. It is a second chance piece of paper."

Then he looks back down at my records and says, "According to what I see, you have had multiple second chances!"

I could hear the Program Directors wife gasping for air as to suggest that she felt something bad was about to happen. My Lawyer didn't say a word and I didn't say a word. The individual who should have spoken on my behalf did not; it was the Commonwealth's Attorney that spoke.

The Commonwealth's Attorney stood up to address the Judge and he said, "Your Honor, I know that we are not accustomed to giving probation or parole to individuals with a record such as Mr. Dukes. Especially to individuals who were awaiting sentencing and have went to a program to benefit himself during their sentencing process. We understand that this happens all the time, but if we look at Mr. Duke's case individually, we can see that this is a gentleman who went to the Salvation Army on his own merit, and according to the Directors, he has maintained good standing with the program. He has become a leader within the program, and he is also scheduled to graduate the program in a couple of weeks. The Salvation Army has offered him a job there.

Now if he is not the type of person that we say we want to help, then I don't know who is. So, we're just asking your Honor if we can give Mr. Dukes one more opportunity, and one more chance."

So, the Judge asked, "Do you have anything to say?"

I just simply told him the truth. I said, "Your Honor, most of my adult life has revolved around substance abuse, even from an early age. Alcohol has been a huge part of my life. There's only a certain amount of blame that I can place at the feet of others, because there became a time when I had to take responsibility for myself. I'm very talented, and I'm very gifted, but I have not learned how to live free. The Salvation Army has given me an opportunity. They have given me trust and they have provided an atmosphere in which I was able to heal spiritually, physically, and mentally. I believe that I deserve another chance, because I am trying to give myself another chance. I hope you can see that if the Commonwealth's Attorney is willing to give me a chance, then I hope that you will give me that same opportunity. I also promise you that you will never see me back in this courtroom again for anything related to drugs or alcohol."

I had much more to say, but I felt that if I said anything else, it would just be the ramblings of a guy trying to get out of going to jail. So that was it. He asked everyone to stand and The Judge took a few more looks at my record and shook his head.

He looked at me and said, "Mr. Dukes, I will accept this plea agreement!"

You could hear the whole courtroom clapping. I wish you could feel the peaceful presence of God that I felt that day you would shout. It wasn't because God has not been with me or has not showed up for me before, it was just the manner of how it happened. It was so profound, and bold that it was in your face. No one could deny that God was with me on that day. I knew it and there was something deep down inside of me that said, "I know I might not be a perfect individual, but I'm moving forward." I know I might not dot every "I" and cross every "T," but I am done with drinking and drugs; I knew it. So, on that day, I went back to the Salvation Army and all eyes were on me.

When I walked through those doors, all the people there were smiling and clapping. Everyone was so proud and so happy that I was given another chance. So, what will I do with it? How would I respond when things went wrong again? Will I turn to drugs and alcohol when people say things that oppose me? Only time will tell, but for today I was okay.

On April 1st, 2011, I Graduated from the Salvation Army Rehabilitation Center. I've actually completed something and that was something I hadn't done in a long time. I was offered a job as an Auctioneer and the Bric and Brac Supervisor. I stayed at the Salvation Army for a few more weeks until I was able to find a place to stay. The auction was still doing great, and we were still breaking records on a weekly basis. It is like I was a professional. It seemed like I was meant to do this. I had always been given a gift with my voice, either doing bad or good. My voice has always been used as a tool to accomplish things. Everything was going pretty well, but it wasn't long before some of the same ole things started to happen. There were a lot of women who would come to the auction, and they have shown great interest in me. I met some really nice women, some very wealthy, some older, some younger, and there were some that I really did liked, but something was eating at me. It kept eating and eating at me. I needed to make an effort to reconcile with my wife. I was in this Christian program and I believed in Christian principles. I was a minister for heaven's sake. I had to give my marriage one more opportunity. I wanted to give it one more chance, because there was such a great peace and forgiveness bestowed upon me, and I know that many of the issues that I had, negatively impacted my marriage were about me. Maybe I can heal. If my healing continues, maybe the healing of my marriage can happen. So, I reached out to my wife to see what we could do? She always thought that we would be back together. She always had a desire that I would come back, because I always did. So much time has passed between us. So many things have transpired; between being in and out of jail, back and forth on the streets and the fight with my stepson. Not to mention the three years I spent in an Arizona Prison. All of these issues really changed everything between us, but nevertheless I tried.

I remembered going home on a visit one day and I saw my wife struggling to walk. She wasn't doing well physically. She wasn't really honest with me about the magnitude of what she was going through, but I could see it. She didn't want to tell me some things that she thought would hinder me from wanting to come home. Even my stepson and I were trying to get along. He came to visit me at the center one time, and he needed some money for something. I had no problem giving it to him. Hell, why would I after all the things that I have taken from him when he wasn't around; just to get a piece of crack or a bottle of alcohol. I caused them to feel so much pain, anger, and resentment toward me, but we tried. So, after my visit, I left around 1 or 2 that afternoon. I was going to get on the bus, but a young lady called me from the auction at the same time I saw one of our neighbors. I waved at the neighbor and by the time I got to the center, the neighbor went and told my wife that I was really smiling while I was talking on the phone. I can't remember who I was talking to at that time, but I was possibly smiling. So, my wife went off and it was a little more than normal. She made phone calls to the people watching the desk and told them all of our personal business. I was so angry, and right or wrong, I felt that I couldn’t go back into that environment. I told her that I didn't want to come back home to that situation. We can’t live in this one-bedroom apartment and my stepson still be there. It wasn't my place to tell her that I'm not coming home if he is still there, because let's be honest, when I'm not there he is the one helping. He is the one taking care of things while I'm on the streets, acting like a damn fool or in prison being fed by the State. All the while, they are struggling at home. So, I can't make that call, but one thing that I must maintain is my peace of mind. If I continue to go back and forth to jail, I'm going to be the one suffering. I'm the only one losing things and everybody else’s life is going to go on. I could possibly lose my life on the streets from the next piece of crack I smoke. I had to make a decision to protect myself, so I just ignored it and I continued to move on as best as I could. It was hard because I was new to this, but I kept moving forward without taking the drink. One of the residents who was manning the phones at the house told me that my wife had called and went on a rampage about the kind of person that I was and the type of life that I lived and all sorts of other things. That almost took me over the edge, because I remembered from past situations, like the one in Arizona and the one in Richmond, where my wife would call people and share my personal information that had nothing to do with them. That always bothered me, and I am facing the same situation again. What am I going to do? I can easily leave the Salvation Army and go back on the streets. I can say f*** everything, but I didn't. I had to make a choice. I had to choose life or death, so I did. I decided that I was done. I decided that the marriage was over. It was one of the hardest decisions that I ever had to make, and it wasn't a popular one. Some people thought that I should have stayed with my wife, because she was sick and that she stayed with me when I was incarcerated. They all had valid points. Some people said that I should give her another chance like God gave you multiple chances. They are valid points, but the only thing that I was concerned about was which decision was going to give me peace. I had a level of peace in my life that I never had before, and I couldn't allow anyone or anything to take it. My wife didn't think I was serious, because I kept coming back. I tried to talk to the Chaplain to see if he would be willing to have a conversation with my wife, stepson, and me. For some reason, he refused to get involved in it. Whatever his reasons were, those we're his reasons. I had a lot of sleepless nights trying to decide, but I realized that I would only be staying out of obligation. I knew that staying would have been destructive for me. I loved my wife, but our marriage was lost, and it was lost years ago. So, it was done, and it was over. I continued to move on the best way I could for the first year. Trying to remain clean, without drinking or without taking drugs, was very hard for me, because I had to deal with so many emotions. I was dealing with the emotions of not having a place to go, not having a job, and a broken marriage. I dealt with the guilt from making that decision, and all the past issues dealing with the people that I hurt. I also had to deal with the fact of knowing that I have been an absent father. I had a lot on my plate mentally, spiritually, and physically. My body was still healing, but I kept moving and I kept going. One day while I was at the auction, a young lady popped up and she said she was looking for a couch.

We were both flirting with each other, nothing serious, but it was just something about her. She was short, cute, and dark-skinned. I could tell that she was a little older than I. She had a nice figure and a nice smile, but she wasn't overly friendly. She was more closed than anything. After that auction was over, I asked her if we could go to the movies. I told her that I didn't have a vehicle, and would she mind coming to pick me up here? I would buy dinner and take her to a movie. Her mother was standing there, and I didn't have any problem whatsoever sharing those things with her in front of her mother. I knew something was going on with me, because I was able to be open and honest regardless of how I might look. When most people meet or date, they try to present themselves in the best manner at the beginning. I just came right out with it. Look, I'm homeless and I live in this shelter right now. I don't have a car, but I would like to take you to the movies and to get something to eat. She agreed and picked me up that Saturday. We went to Hardee's, had something to eat, and then we went to go see the Avengers. Anyone who knows me, knows that I'm a huge Marvel Comics fan. You will know more about that later on in the story. It was very important for me to go see the Avengers movie, because it was the first time that all these heroes have gotten together in a huge movie like this. So, while we were eating dinner, I told her all about myself. I told her about how many times I've been incarcerated and how I abused and used drugs. I talked about how I wanted to live a different life. I also told her that I'm still legally married and she just looked at me and took it all in. Then I told her what I wanted to do in life. I wanted to go to school, get my driver's license, volunteer in my community, and overall, just be a better person. I just want to grow. I don't want to go back to jail and prison anymore. I don't want to sleep under bridges or eat out of a trash can. I just want to be in peace and try to help someone else get out of the situations I was in. She said okay and that was it. We had a beautiful time at the movies, and it was probably one of the best dates that I ever been on, because I was free. I was at peace with someone that I was interested in and I was doing something that I loved.

The next day was Sunday. When I called her that morning, I found out she had been crying. She had lost her father so I asked her to pick me up from the center so that I could spend some time with her. She came to pick me up and she took me back to her house. She had only been there a couple of weeks herself and was trying to get things together. She had shared with me that she had been in a relationship that wasn't very healthy, so she was in the process of starting over too. Now, here is this woman's crying out to a perfect stranger, but she's crying out to a person who is very familiar with pain. She had lost her father and her father hadn't been in her life. I don't even know if she ever met him or even had a conversation with him, but she was crying for a man that she didn't know. I couldn't imagine the pain that she was in, but I can relate to losing a parent. So, we just held each other and talked. Then one thing led to another and we ended up making love to each other. It was beautiful and it was nice. It was needed for both of us, but none of us knew what was going to transpire in the future for us. Was I using her for a temporary release or was she using me for temporary satisfaction? Neither one of us knew the answer that day, but we did need each other at that time. May 12th was Mother's Day which is also my birthday. She came and picked me up and took me to her house. I made her a huge dinner for Mother's Day. Yes, on my birthday, I really can't focus or celebrate on my birthday because it is usually always the day before Mother's Day or the day after Mother's Day or a couple of days before or after. It's always about the mothers. Mother's Day is always rough on me because of how I lost my mother. My mother's death has not left me, and it is still a big part of who I am. It is still a part of my healing process and at this particular time, I really don't know how big of an issue my mother's death was to me, but as time went on, I found out. Now we are a couple of weeks into this relationship and I'm dealing with a lot of issues as far as where I'm going to live. Should I go find a halfway house or a clean and sober living house to stay at? I couldn't stay at the Salvation Army for much longer, and my marriage was done. I knew that the streets were definitely out of the question, but then I had an issue with continuing this relationship with this woman while I was still married. A lot of people were weighing in on the subject one way or the other. If it makes you happy that's all that matters. Well if it is God's will for you to be with her, he will make a way for you to be with her. You can't open one door unless you close another door.

Once again, they were all valid points, but I was starting to realize, especially from having been a License Ordained Minister and all those years of preaching, that I cannot live my life based on the rudiments, traditions, and interpretations of other men. I have to live my life for what is peaceful to me. So, I had a long talk with Jackie about it; the idea of me moving in with her. I also had to consider some other things also. When people are in recovery it is always suggested to not get involved in relationship within one year. That's a suggestion not a commandment. I didn't know her, and I didn't know her history. I've only known this lady for a couple of weeks. The same goes true for her, now, no one in their right mind would allow a man at a homeless shelter, with a criminal record to come and live with them after only knowing them for a couple of weeks. It just didn't make sense for either one of us, especially for her in my opinion. After we had that conversation, I could not sleep a wink. I was tossing and turning, because I didn't know what to do. I was stressing and I just asked God to show me the direction that I need to go. When I woke up the next morning, a great peace fell over me and I called Jackie. I told her that I think we should live together.

She said, "Okay, let's just do it!"

So, with all the baggage that we both have, we decided to live together after knowing each other for just 21 days. Now that might sound very crazy to a lot of people and I would understand why but let me be honest with you; I would not recommend that to anyone. I would not suggest or encourage that to anyone. It goes against all principles and traditions that I've ever taught, but what I was supposed to do? I moved out of the Salvation Army and the Director's wife was not very happy with me. Her attitude towards me changed greatly even though I was doing an excellent job. I was running the whole Warehouse, and I was no longer the Bric-A-Brac Supervisor. I had moved up to the Expediting Supervisor and I was also running the forklifts and driving trucks in the parking lot. I was also calling the auction and the only employee every morning that would go into the meeting room with all the guys for the morning motivations. I would go to listen and occasionally I would share.

I would give back, because I was only a few weeks out of graduation myself. Just because I had a job didn't mean I was too far from them. I was still apart of them, and the men on the facility loved me, but it seemed that the Leadership wasn't loving me as much as they were. Every time certain jobs would become open, and I was more than qualified for or it was my turn to be considered for, I was told that my record would hinder me from getting the job. If you apply for it the front office might send word back to let you go. So, we don't want to take that chance. I knew that the Salvation Army had been a blessing to me, and that the Director and his wife played a major role in getting me where I am today, but I still felt neglected. I felt that I needed more and that I had more to give. I decided that I wanted to go to school. So, while I was at the Salvation Army and I was living with Jackie, I decided to go to school. I signed up for J. Sergeant Reynolds Community College. I decided to study Substance Abuse Counseling, and Human services. What else would I take up? I know more about drugs than I did about anything else. I went to work 8 hours a day and I went to school twice a week at night. I also had an online class. I was doing it! I was living, and I was healing. Doors started opening for me to go back to one of the prisons that I was incarcerated, but it was a women's facility on Courthouse Road. I had to make a decision, because this was a church service so I had to tell the Leadership there that there's nothing I would rather do more than to come and be a part of the fellowship, but I'm living with someone and we are not married. I don't know how you guys are going to handle that and I don't even know how I am going to handle that, but that is the situation. So, they told me that they would get back to me. I was working in the auction one day and there was a couple called the Smiths, who were very, very, close to me. They saw my struggles and they saw me when I came in the program. They also knew some of my history. They used to help me out a lot and they were very kind. Even to this day I still consider them very close friends. I would share my personal issues with them. I shared with Mrs. Smith (a very devout Christian) that I had an opportunity to go to the prison, but I felt like I shouldn't because I worried about what people would say about me and my living conditions.

I live with Jackie and we are not married. She looked me right in my eyes and asked, "Do you have something to say to them?"

I said, "Yes I do have something to say to them."

She said, "We'll say it!"

I just looked at her and once again the peace came upon me to tell my story. Not that I shouldn't straighten out certain things or move forward to correct certain things in my life, but the peace came from making the decision not to be quiet based on my circumstances, but to speak my truth about what God has done in my life regardless of my circumstances. I made a choice that I would start going back to the prisons which would be the beginning of my volunteer work. The days at the Salvation Army were getting very old for me. I was tired of feeling like a second-class citizen. I got tired of the side eyes that I would get from the Program Directors wife and I've done nothing but be kind and considerate. I continually try to be a role model and a leader, but she just kept treating me like crap; at least that's how I felt. So, I had another decision to make. Once again, tradition and good common sense always tells us that you don't ever leave a job unless you have another one was contemplating leaving, but where would I go? I didn't have another job, I had a record, and I didn't have many employable skills that people were looking for, but there was something that I noticed I was good at, while working in the Auction. I was always good at talking to people. I was good at getting people to show me things. I was also good at selling people things. Many people who came to the auction had their own businesses. They would either go to flea markets or they had their own storefront. Many of them did very well and they worked for themselves. It was very appealing to me because I was getting to a certain age. I didn't want to work in the freezing cold warehouse during the wintertime or the blazing heat during the summer. I had to remember that I wasn't that far away from sleeping under a bridge or being in a jail cell. So, I had to be very careful in my decision making. I was living with this woman who was taking care of most of the bills because I didn't make much at The Salvation Army. The money that I got from school was always a big help, but I needed, and I wanted to do more.

I was never content with people telling me what I cannot do or obtain because of my past. I was tired of allowing that to dictate my life. My past was no longer going to be an obstacle for me. I was going to take my past and use it as a steppingstone. With some counsel from some people that I knew, I started going to a couple of flea markets in the area. There was one in my neighborhood called the Supreme Flea Market. I went in there a couple times and I really liked the vibe of the place. There was an older couple that ran it. The place didn't have a lot of traffic, but the atmosphere was right and that was mainly because of her. She was so sweet, kind and inviting. They were more African eccentric people. He sold African products and she cooked. The atmosphere was just alluring, and I had a conversation with Jackie, who also used to like and go to the flea market. She would go buy items and post them on social media and sell them. We had the bright idea to create our own business. I would use all the information that I gained from the Salvation Army; work ethic, personality, and my mouthpiece to move forward to learn new things. I also learned that everybody is not always pleased with what you are excited about, but nevertheless, I made the decision to move on from the Salvation Army. It seemed like everyone was upset to see me go, but the Program Director's wife. She didn't really care at least that's how I felt. It was really a big step but how will I know if I'm going to succeed if I never step out on faith. The flea markets are not a reliable income. One week I might make $1,000. One day I might make $1,000, and in one month, I might not make $100, but I was ready to move on faith, because I knew that I was destined do something greater. I'm not saying that working at the Salvation Army was not a great blessing because it was something to be thankful for. I'm grateful for the fact that I recognized it was time to go. During the final company meeting with all the supervisors, everyone shared their goodbyes, congratulations, and well wishes with me. When it got to the Program Director, he gave me a very well send off and he said some very nice things, but his wife didn't say a word. As I reflect on this, there's only two reasons why I felt that she was treating me like this. One is that when I was working as a Clothing Room Supervisor, we had a very challenging gentleman. His name was Charles, and he was complaining about working on a particular day or something of that sort. He kept complaining about the program and I told him why it was so important to comply with the rules and everything.

The Program Director's wife walked in and I said," You don't have to take it from me. You can ask her."

Charles went on to ask her and she gave him her answer and she looked at me and walked off. Later on, I heard that she was upset because she felt like I didn't defend her while that gentleman was talking, but what she didn't know was that I spent the past 30 minutes, prior to her walking in, defending the whole place. I didn't say anything because he wasn't talking to me. He was talking to her. She was in charge, and he didn't get in her face or touch her. He spoke his mind and she spoke hers. I heard that she was upset with me about that, and the fact that she felt I was wrong in how I ended my marriage and that I was living with someone else. Whichever the case, I had to come to peace with the fact that regardless of how this woman treated me, God still used her as a vessel to help me get to where I am now. I have never forgotten the Salvation Army and on many occasions, I tried to go back. I tried to share some stories and experiences with some of the guys. I asked to come back to volunteer and do some teaching, but they wouldn't allow it. I had left a newspaper that did a story on me and one of the guys at the center had obtained it. He had hung it up on one of the bulletin boards so the guys could see something positive from the alumni of the program. When she found out that it was me on the bulletin board, she took it down. Now I don't know how true that is, but I don't believe that's too far from the truth. Nevertheless, I wish them well and I'm grateful for all that the Salvation Army had done for me, but that chapter is now closed.

teractive Hip-Hop and R&
POWE
rRichmond.con

# NEW LIFE

Life outside of the Salvation Army was very scary. I really didn't know what I was doing. This was my first time trying to really live a life with the mindset that I was not going to get high or drink. I'm in a new relationship, a new house and I'm trying a new career. I'm trying to live a life that I have never lived before. I'm still full of pain and guilt, but I still have a ton of hope stored up inside of me, because of all that God has been showing me lately. I really don't know who I am and I'm waking in this new reality. I really want to change. I want to speak to people. I want to go inside of the prisons and jails. I want to go to the recovery facilities, and I want to go to school. I want to do all of these things, but I really needed to know how to live. So, the Supreme Flea Market is the place that allowed me to come in and set up shop. I only had two small sections in the beginning. I sold used items from electronics, clothing, to appliances and many other things. I didn't really know what I was doing, but I knew how to talk to people. I knew that I liked electronics and Jackie also loved the idea, even though she was working a full-time job elsewhere. She would love to come in and go buy items and set them up. She loves that aspect of it, but it was really up to me to run the business. I was the one who had the time and we tried to make money from this venture, and we did well. The money was very inconsistent, but it allowed me to see that I had a talent for this. The flea market didn't have a lot of traffic so most of the customers that I had come from my ability to use Facebook. I would join certain groups on Facebook like yard sales and buy and sell groups in the area. Each group could have from 1,000 to 10,000 members. I would take my items and post them. I would tell them where I'm located and tell them that I'm willing to negotiate on every item and people would flow into the flea market just to see me. Then they would get an idea of where the flea market was located. So other vendors where benefiting from my efforts as well. Many people who came didn't even know the flea market existed until they came in from one of my posts. It was always frustrating to me that the leadership at the time didn't see that or just didn't care.

He was a good man and his wife was a beautiful person, but we can all get stuck in our ways and only see things the way we want to see them. I stayed in the flea market and I continue to learn. The one thing that I admired about the flea market was that it was all black owned and they would always try to promote blackness. The main shop at the flea market was called Afrikongo, which the owner ran. They always wanted to promote Afrocentric qualities, events, fashion shows, concerts, and things of that nature. One of my pet peeves at that place was how people would put so much energy into promoting an event but won't even come and open they're shops on time, especially on Saturday which has always been the busiest day at a flea market. Hell, Saturday is the busiest day in retail businesses in most cases. How would you like to walk into a facility that opens up at 10 a.m. and there's only one person open? That was the frustration that I had with this place, because I tried to do what I could to try and make the place grow, even on my own, with all the people that I could bring in. I was just one person and I could only do so much. If we could just get everybody to come in on time that one day. We could have some consistency on the busiest day, but that's another story. The flea market did provide financial assistance for me at the time. It gave me an opportunity to learn and grow into a different individual and allowed me to develop more leadership skills and I had my own business. I was a small business owner and I was proud of it. Regardless of the issues that I had with the flea market, one thing that was undeniable, in my opinion, was how they loved people. They love the flea market and I wanted it to become a cultural epicenter in the city. They were very kind to me and gave me many opportunities to learn and grow, even when I couldn't pay the rent on time. I wish them continued success in all they do, and I hope the Supreme Flea Market will be blessed without measure. I did fairly well, and it was mainly because of Facebook, but as I was using Facebook as a tool to promote my business, it became one of the most important aspects of my life. That might sound crazy to a lot of people, but Facebook gave me the opportunity, after years of being in and out of prison, and after years of being on the streets and sleeping under bridges, to connect and reach people who were in Portsmouth.

People that I might have went to school with. I remember it was amazing to me that I was able to see these people that I remembered. To my surprise and hurt, I found that many people thought I was dead or in prison. Facebook became my life, but it also came with issues. With all the multitude of friends that I was able to connect with, most of them were from Portsmouth. I lived in Richmond and out of a thousand friends, maybe 10 of them were from Richmond. I was also connecting with a lot of women and I would be lying if I said that I wasn't being flirtatious or saying some things that I shouldn't have said on Facebook, but Jackie helped me learn that lesson really quick. My selfishness was rising up again, because it was always about me. I got high because I wanted to. I got drunk because I wanted to. I lied and stole because I wanted to. For whatever the reason, it was all about my selfishness. It was addictive to have all the attention that I was getting from these women. Many of the women wouldn't have given me the time of day when I was younger. Back then, they were known as some of the most popular and beautiful girls from Cavalier Manor. They were now in my inbox, and now they we're trying to get my attention and much more. Some were bold enough to ask for sex, money and I was even asked to come live with them. Jackie and I had some very bad arguments over Facebook. So, I had to make a serious decision on what role Facebook was going to play in my life. I'm still working on it. Thank God it's not on that level anymore, but it's far from being a perfect situation. Facebook also allowed me to connect with my father's side of the family. It also allowed me a voice for my political opinions. I would normally put quotes up and do Facebook live. I created a little saying called *Stay out of Egypt*, because I wanted to help someone. I hoped someone was able to hear my message and I hoped someone was going to be free from it, but it was really so that I can remember where I came from. Egypt was a big part of my life and a bigger part of my past. I couldn't forget how I lived, dressed, ate, and dwelled in Egypt. My whole life was about Egypt and now I was in the process of coming out. Everything in my life was about trying to remember how to stay out of Egypt. I didn't always do it successfully, but I did not drink, and I did not get high. Some of the greatest challenges for me was trying to learn how to live free.

Life still happens, bills still have to be paid, and holidays still come up. How will I function? Jackie had a family that was huge, and I grew up with just a mother and a father until my mother passed away at a very early age. Jackie had brothers, sisters, aunts, uncles, and a multitude of cousins, nieces, and nephews. I remember the very first time that I went to one of her family functions. I was so nervous; not only because alcohol was going to be present, but how was I was going to deal with all of these people? How would they deal and respond to me? What if they asked me are we married? What if they asked me what are all my plans? What am I going to say? I thought that I would try to be myself, because people will always judge me for one thing or another. Some judge because I speak a certain way, or they think that I'm this great Christian. Others think I'm too intelligent or that I'm not black enough, and others only know the trifling, alcoholic, drunk. There is no midway with me. So, I decided that I'm just going to live my life and be at peace with who I am. I really don't know who this guy is yet, but I'm not going to try and live up to everybody's expectations about who they think I should be. Let me just live today and be at peace and see how this goes. So, I ended up getting through multiple parties and multiple events without drinking. One of the greatest challenges was a place called the Virginia Beach Funk Fest that was held every August. When I first went to that event, it was heart shattering. I always loved old school music from Prince, Cameo, Earth, Wind, and Fire to the Gap Band and Parliament. The Funk Fest was designed to promote this type of music on a weekend for free every summer. Who wouldn't want to go to a free funk concert on the beach? I didn't know how I was going to respond to this. I always wanted to go early so that I could get a good seat. You had to go early in the morning to set up and you had to deal with the heat. It was hot, I was thirsty, and I was hungry, but I was having a great time. As the time drew near, the main event started. I believe it was Confunkshun that year. People started dancing and I could look around and see a whole sea of people just enjoying themselves. Some of them dancing, some drinking, some singing, some of them sleeping. People were living life and it was something that I haven't experienced in a mighty long time. People take life for granted.

People go to these events every year and don't seem to grasp the magnitude of how special this is. Just being able to sit and enjoy yourself. There was no fighting or fussing. It was nothing, but black people on the beach having fun. Now this was Virginia Beach, if you can understand the significance of what I just said. I started to learn how to live, because it wasn't long ago when Jackie and I first started seeing each other. We would go down to the James River and I remember she made a video of me taking my shoes off and putting my feet in the water and everybody was out there. Some sunbathing, some swimming, and people are just having fun. She made a video of me and later that day I watched the video. The guy that I was watching didn't recognize who he was, even though I knew it was me. He had on the same clothing that I did, and he had the same look that I did and he had the same build that I did, but he didn't have the same expression that I normally would have on my face. It was a person who was sitting on the rocks of a river looking out into the river and just experiencing peace. I looked at the video over and over again. The look that I saw on that guy's face was peace. I never recognize this look on my face before. It was something that was so strange to me. It was so out of character for me to have this look, but it was there. Tubby, this 13-year-old boy, has found peace. What he found he vowed that he would never let it go again regardless of what someone else said or did. Regardless of the situations or circumstances in life, he would not allow anyone take his peace again. He almost lost his life and many other things for this peace. So, at this particular moment, this is the most valuable asset that he has. Today it is still the most valuable asset.

This was the first time in my life that I could ever say that I truly found some peace. My relationship with Jackie isn't the perfect relationship, but what relationship was? Her family embraced me, and they knew some of my past, but no one ever came up to me bugging and badgering me. They all accepted me, because all they really cared about was that their family member was happy. We moved on and continued to grow. We went to church and meetings together. We experienced things that we both have never experienced before. We went on vacations and different events in different cities and different states. I've had some good women in my past and I've had some great women in my past, but the one thing that I regret is that they all looked and hoped to see the man that Jackie is living with every day. One of the things I would always tell Jackie was that we are here to help each other heal. Jackie was able to show me things that I wasn't used to doing. Maybe some women in my past wanted to show me, but I wasn't interested, or I was too caught up in trying to get drunk and high. She showed me how to manage money. She showed me how to make sure the bills are paid on time. She showed me how to be consistent on living which is something that I've never done before. I believe that I gave her elements of hope, strength, and motivation, because she would tell me on many occasions that when I spoke about all my goals and dreams and to see them being fulfilled, amazes her, because it seems like nothing holds me down. This is where things get tricky, because I've been here before. I've been in a place where I'm doing good and trying to move forward. Something has to be different this time, but as of right now I'll just keep moving forward.

School is going pretty well and somewhere along the line, the little, young fella in high school who failed two grades has now managed to obtain a 4.0 grade point average. I was on the Dean's List and the President's List. I was entered into the Honors Society and I was always able to share my story with my classmates. They were truly amazed at how far I've come. Soon it became a time for me to do an internship and I had to decide on where I would like to go. Since I was studying for a Human Services Degree and a Substance Abuse Counseling Certificate, I thought it'll be fruitful for me to try to intern somewhere where my interests lie. I called many places, but I didn't get much feedback in the timely manner, but I was able to secure an internship at The Healing Place. I had an opportunity to get interviewed by a lady named Carolyn, who ran the family section of a company called Caritas. There was an opening in the Sober Up Center section. A place where guys would come in and try to detox from whatever drugs they were on, and then they would have an opportunity at the end of their detox to either come into the program or perhaps utilize the other section of the program which is an overnight shelter. I thought this was a huge opportunity for me, because it wasn't long ago that I had to utilize this facility. I came in on multiple occasions, because I was tired or needed some help or whatever the case might have been. I tried to complete the program a couple of times. When I felt like I was clean and healthy enough or when things had gotten smoothed over with my wife, it was time to go back home. So, I never completed the program, but I learned so much from it with the constant educational aspect of it. You can't help but be bombarded by information concerning substance abuse and self-help techniques. They planted very important seeds in my life that I still apply today. So here I was, an intern about to sit behind a desk at the Sober Up Center. It was an amazing experience. I would write in the logbook, check blood pressures and helped the gentlemen who were coming in. Some of which I've known from my drugging days. I would have to make sure that I was able to monitor the people who are there, because some people really had come in bad shape. Some of them could possibly die from a bad detox. There was a lady named Miss Patricia. She was one of the nicest people I have ever met. She ran the Sober Up Center. I shared with her that I used to be in this facility.

She asked me, "Can I pull your picture?"

Everyone who comes through the door has to have a picture taken. I gave her my name and my picture popped up. Now Miss Patricia had been working at the facility for a long time and she has seen many people come and go. She has seen some of the worst conditions that that anyone could ever imagine, but when my first picture popped up, she looked at the picture and looked at me. Then looked back at the picture again and looked back at me and all she could say was Lord have mercy. I asked if I could take a picture of that picture. I did and I still keep it with me today. I was a 130 pounds, bald headed and I looked just like an alien. My face was sunk in from the crack that I had smoked. My head was big on top and I had a burn mark on my lip from putting the crack pipe backwards in my mouth. I was so full of despair, pain, and lack of hope. That picture became a tool for me when I would go to the prisons, recovery facilities or talk to other groups. Somewhere around my third week, a lot of interest was made concerning my employment there. I thought to myself what a nice job. What a beautiful job to work in a recovery facility, because there is a gentleman named Mr. Jeffrey.

He always said, “I'm in recovery and I work in recovery. What a beautiful thing!”

I thought I had an opportunity for that. What a great opportunity it would be for me to be able to work at this facility. I was excited and I was interested, and everyone was okay with it. Ms. Carolyn was okay with it and I was okay with it, so they advised me to go and talk to Mr. Jackson.

One day, Mr. Jackson asked, “Do you have a felony?”

I said, “Yes sir!”

He said, “We can't go any further. We can't use you. I'm sorry but that's just the way it is!”

Mr. Jackson was the program director and one of the best men I ever met, but on that particular day I was crushed. I just kept hanging in there, but I was losing faith to be honest. My internship was about to end, and when it was over, I thanked everybody for the experience, and I moved on. I was still at the flea market and working on my final semester for school. Then one day out of the blue, Miss Carolyn had called me about a position that was opening at Caritas. I was excited about it, but I can't remember exactly what the position was. I was a full-time student, I had a little thrift store inside of a flea market, and I was doing great in school. I was also doing community service work and volunteering in the community. I was waiting and looking for some type of breakthrough while I was in this process. Miss Carolyn set up an interview and I went and had a meeting with everyone that was necessary. I didn't get that job either. It was very discouraging, and I was starting to think that regardless of my actions, and what I do, my past is just going to be a hindrance for me. I felt like giving up on many occasions. How many no’s am I going to have to hear? I am trying and I'm doing my best not to drink or get high. I'm not hanging on street corners; I'm just trying my best to move forward, but I keep hearing no. Jackie would always encourage me and tell me things are going to be better and I would try to hang on. I tried to be a light and tell other people to hang on, but I just wasn't feeling it.

Miss Carolyn called me again and she wanted me to come and apply for an overnight shelter position with the families. She wanted me to come on a Saturday. Saturday was a business day for me at the flea market. I didn't really want to waste my Saturday going in for a job interview with the same people who told me no a couple of weeks earlier, but something told me in my heart and spirit to go. I went to the interview and it went very well. See, I never had a problem selling myself because I know who I am, and I know what I bring to the table. I know what I'm capable of, but it's always about my past. Will somebody give me a chance to show them that I'm not that person anymore? This was the position for the families. I would go in on Friday night to pack up the families so that they could be transported to the next shelter site on Saturday. The families could consist of one lady that's pregnant to a family of 10. I got the job and I was very proud. I was very happy, and I was glad to be a part of the team. I met my new co-workers and received training to begin working. That job showed me a lot about who I am and how much growing up I needed to do, because I was going to school at night on Tuesdays and Thursdays. I was still trying to run a store from Wednesday to Sunday. The greatest challenges were Fridays and Saturdays. Friday mornings I would go to the auction to find items to sell for my store on Saturday. I would get the items, come back to my store, clean them, test them, post them, set them up, and leave the store. I'd go to work at 3 p.m. and stay up all night until 7 in the morning, then come home change clothes and go to the flea market at 10 a.m. and stay until 4:05 p.m. There were some days and some weekends that were very rough on me because I was very tired. I was able to sleep some nights at the shelter after things calmed down, but there were some nights when sleeping wasn't possible. You could have seen a fight, or somebody could have gotten sick and the ambulance might have to be called. Sometimes the conditions of the place didn't allow for good night's rest. Being a man around a lot of women was challenging also. There were some women there who were very attractive, but they were in a situation. I would be lying if I said that some of them didn't come at me pretty hard, which also showed me that I was not as strong as I thought I was. As an individual, I still needed to grow up, and I still need to learn how to be a better person.

I know how to manipulate and function in selfishness and just because I'm no longer drinking or getting high does not mean that I have made it or that I am this great individual. That job did have some challenges for me, but most of the ladies really appreciated me and most of the kids adored me, because I love kids. I would often pull the guys together who were there or the young boys and give them some words of encouragement. I would often share my story to let them know how important it is to hold on and keep the faith. I knew that Caritas wasn't going to be long-term, but there were a couple things that transpired that made me feel that it was getting closer for me to go. When it seemed like an opportunity wasn't going to be, it opened for me. Things that I thought I could do with that operation or job, it seemed liked my record would hinder that. When it was time to do a background check, regardless of my skills, and desire, when it came back that I had a certain felony, it closed. I didn't want to be stuck in the position my whole existence with this company, working at an overnight shelter. Now, I'm not saying I wasn't grateful and thankful for that opportunity. That opportunity opened doors for me that wouldn't have opened if I was not there, but I knew that I wanted to do more and then one day, things changed for me at Caritas. A young lady accused me of coming in a bathroom and assaulting her. Now, I believe this occurred around 2017. The atmosphere surrounding men and sexual abuse was very high and I was very afraid, not because I did that, but because I was a black man in America with a long criminal record. I knew that I didn't touch that woman and most of the people who I worked with knew that. I also had people who corroborated my version of the story. The challenge for me was managing my emotions and how I would deal with this publicly, because I want to do so much in the community. How would I be perceived if this kind of information gets out? I wouldn't know what to do, but by the grace of God it was found that I didn't do it. I was able to move on from that incident, but things felt different after that. I was scared to walk around certain women and I was scared to look at them in fear that it would be taken the wrong way. I was so caught up on what other people thought that I could hardly function. I was worried about who was going to call and even when I went to places to speak, I would think that they knew something about it. I was really going through a great deal. I even contemplated drinking.

See, one of the most important things about coming out of Egypt is when certain things happen in your life, you have to be honest enough to look at the role that you played in it. Even though I did not go in the bathroom and touch that woman, I had to look at any role that I might have played in it. How did I talk to this woman? How was I talking to other women? Was I more flirtatious than professional? So, I had to really look at that whole picture. I had to use it as an opportunity to grow, because if I allowed my feelings and emotions to dictate my next step and direction, I would have been drinking and drugging. So, with a lot of support, reflection, and healing I got through it. It seemed as if my days at Caritas were getting to an end. I wanted more and I didn't want to experience another situation like that all because a woman got angry with you. I had nowhere to go so I just prayed and walked cautiously from then on. To my dismay, more storms were brewing. Trying to get through life during tough times without drinking and using drugs was very difficult for anyone who has used for the majority of their life. The things that most people would consider to be minimal or just another walk in the park were gigantic mountains for people like me. There is no greater example then when I was trying to get my driver's license. This was a monumental task for me seeing that I haven't had a driver's license in years, let alone a car, but things were going well, and I had got a little time under my belt. I was working a job. I owned a business. I was going to school and I was getting scholarship money, grants, and loans. So, I decided to find out how much it would cost for me to get a license. There was no way in the world that I would ever be able to drive again in the state of Virginia because of the huge amount of fines that I owed. I went to DMV and I got a compliance form. It was one of the things that I needed in order to get a license. I had to go to Richmond and Portsmouth courts and make arrangements for my fines. I had to petition both courts to see if I could get a temporary driver's license and I had to make a payment plan with an agency to get it. Now all these things were time-consuming and costly. I had to go before the Judge and ask for the opportunity to get my driver's license wasn't the easiest thing to do because of my criminal and driving history.

This was the first time that I ever went before a Judge to speak from a positive aspect; to speak about the things that I'm doing and share how my life has changed and why I needed my driver's license. All this so I can make more positive strides in my life. Miraculously, the judge granted me a temporary driver's license. Really, What! I haven't had a driver's license in decades. I felt that was a huge step and I was very proud of that. So, with all the paperwork that I got from the courts and all the receipts I got from the company that I made a payment plan with, I went to DMV after a good three to four-month process. When I was finally called to the desk I proceeded to the lady with great pride. I put down all my paperwork and receipts in front of her. She got on the computer and I told her that I wanted to get my license. She punched a few keys and looked at screen and then she said, "Are you prepared to pay your uninsured motorist fee?"

I said, "Yes ma'am!"

I believe the fee was somewhere around $300. She took my card and swiped it and then gave it back to me. I had such a great rush of emotion, and a great sense of accomplishment about something I didn't think would ever happen in the state of Virginia. Then the worker looked at me and said," Sir, have you ever been to Arizona?"

I said, "Yes Mam."

She said, "It's says here that you have a traffic issue and you're not going to be able to get a driver's license here, until you take care of this issue."

I felt the blood in my body start to boil and I didn't know what to do or what to say.

So, I lashed out at the worker, "Why didn't you tell me this before you took my money? Did you see this on the screen prior to taking my money?"

She told me that she was just following procedure and she said, "You need to contact Arizona and find out what the issue is."

I stormed out of the DMV heated. I was mad as I have ever been in over 15 or 20 years.

When I stormed out, I walked right past the car that Jackie was waiting for mean in. She looked at me and saw that something wasn't right. I just walked right past the car and I kept going.

She looked at me and asked, "Where are you going? What's wrong?"

I said, "Just leave me the hell alone!"

I kept walking and just that quick, all hope, peace, godliness, and spirituality went out the door. I was angry and there was only one thing left for me to do. That was to find a store and get something to drink.

I kept walking down the street as she was driving beside me begging me to get in the car yelling, "What the hell is wrong with you? Get your ass in this car!"

I just kept walking and I didn't want to hear anything from anybody, but eventually I got in the car. I finally told her what the problem was she sat quiet because she knew I was very upset and angry.

There's really nothing she could say, but she eventually said, "Well, just call Arizona and see what happens."

I didn't say anything. I just sat in the car and I contemplated, just let me get drunk. Let me get high for one minute. I'm angry enough, and hell, I've been working hard. I've been trying, and I've been trying. It seems like every time I try to do something positive; I get smacked in the face. So, when I finally got home, I sat down to cool off a little bit and I made a phone call to Arizona. While speaking with one of the clerks, she informed me that I owed $10 for some type of track traffic violation that I had when I was driving one of those cars

She said, "Pay the $10 and take a driving improvement course in Richmond and you'll be able to get your license."

I said, "Thank you ma'am," and I hung up the phone. I had turned a little molehill into a huge mountain. All I had to do was pay $10 and sign up to take an 8-hour course on driving improvement.

I was about to throw away everything because of my anger. I was about to allow my emotions to steal my joy. I was about to allow circumstances and situations bring me back to Egypt. I was willing to go back through all the pain that I have experienced. I was willing to throw away every relationship that God has put in my life. I was willing to throw away my freedom all because something didn't go the way that I wanted it to. I paid off the fine and signed up for a drivers improvement course for the following Saturday. The next week, I went back to the DMV with all my proper paperwork, took the test and got my temporary driver's license. What a lesson learned and a huge testimony. What a great blessing to be functioning and to have something in my possession that I never thought I would have in my lifetime. Alcohol almost took that away. It wasn't long after that I learned another lesson in the form of my first vehicle in years. Now that I had a driver's license, maybe I can get some kind of vehicle. I just needed something that I could take my items back and forth from the auction to the flea market and then transport myself back and forth to school and work. So, the next time I got financial aid from school, I decided that I would make some sacrifices and get a vehicle. I decided to go to an auction that someone referred me to. I went to the auction at 3 p.m. I was able to walk around and look at the various cars that would be for sale. The auction didn't start until six and I saw a truck I believe to be a GMC. The floorboards were torn up and there was no radio, but the car started up and the transmission seemed good. I felt that this might be a safe bet to bid on, because no one wanted a truck that look like this. I just wanted something reliable regardless of whatever else was there. I was going to focus on this particular vehicle. After 3 hours of waiting, it was time for the auction to start. The auctioneer was calling out his cadence with professional precision and many people are gathered around in hope to get a good deal on a car. I waited, and I waited, and my car never came through. I started to get nervous, angry and a little anxious, because all these cars were going past and some of them went for very little money and I was missing out on them. My car never came through and I asked the auctioneer," Do you know anything about this particular car?"

He said, "No sir, I'm just calling the auction. You're going to have to go to the front office."

I went up to the front office and asked, "Do you know anything about this particular car?"

They said, "No sir. You're going to have to go back on the yard where all the guys have the cars at."

I walked all the way back to the yard while the auction was going on to ask the guys if they knew anything about the car that I was waiting on and why it hadn't gone through. One of the gentlemen plainly told me that they lost the key and that was when I lost it!

"What do you mean you lost the key? I test drove the car earlier and I've been here since 3 p.m. I've been waiting and waiting for this vehicle!"

They just kept saying," We're sorry, but we can't do anything about it."

In my frustration, I walked back up to the auctioneer as he was calling the auction. People were everywhere and said, "Sir I need to talk to you about this car!"

He said, "Sir, I'm trying to call an auction!"

Jackie was standing next to me looking at me like I had lost my mind. Now, mind you, Jesus has left the building. All that God stuff has left the building. All my spiritual principles have left the building. It's just me, my selfishness, and my self-centeredness standing there fussing and arguing over the car that I wanted.

So, the auctioneer in his frustration said," Sir if you want to bid on the car, bid on a car."

I just threw my hands up in frustration and he said, "Sold!"

Then it felt like the world had stopped and as I looked around. I realized that I had purchased a car with a rejection sticker on it. I was like, oh my God, how could I be so stupid? Jackie is looking at me like I was the most ignorant man on the planet and at that particular time I felt like it. There was nothing I could do so I walked over to the Administrative Office and started to fill out the paperwork for the car that I just purchased with a rejection sticker on it.

Just then, one of the gentlemen who worked in the yard ran to the office and said, "We found the key to that car!"

I looked at him like I wanted to kill him. I really wanted to choke the life out of him, and all of a sudden yall find the key. I just bought this damn car with a rejection sticker on it. Nevertheless, I took the car home. I was still frustrated and sick to my stomach over what I had allowed myself to go through. Once again, I have allowed my emotions to take over and run my life. I have done this on so many other occasions in my life. The next day I drove the car to one of the automotive shops across the street from the flea market. I dropped it off with them and asked could they get it inspected and let me know what's wrong with it. I walked across the street to the flea market to open up my shop and go about my business. I was just praying, Lord, please don't let these people call me and tell me that I'm going to have to spend a fortune on this vehicle.

Two hours later, one of the mechanics called me and said, "Mr. Dukes, your car is ready. Your car passed inspection. You just needed a little bulb. It'll be $16."

I said, "Excuse me, are you sure?"

He said, "Yes sir!"

I said, "There's nothing wrong with the car?"

He said, "No sir, it passed inspection."

I said, "Are you positive?"

He said, "Yes!"

I said, "Okay, I'll be over shortly, and thank you."

So, as I sat in the flea market contemplating what had just happened. It seems that I had bought a 2002, white Mercedes-Benz ML500 Truck for a $1,000, and nothing was wrong with it! I was sitting there asking God, "What part of the game is this?"

There has to be something wrong with this car, but the mechanic said there's nothing wrong with it. I prayed for some type of clarity or understanding. I know that many people might disagree with this and that's on them, but this is what I believe God was trying to say to me. God was trying to say that if you had got the vehicle that you wanted, you had something to do with it, but when people see you in this vehicle, they will know that I had something to do with it. I smiled and said to myself, okay I get it now. Now honestly, any vehicle that I call my own would be a miraculous undertaking, but when I drive into certain places and I see some of the people who used to see me sleeping on the street at 130 pounds and one breath away from death, and see their eyes magnify, is jaw dropping. It's not just because they see me in a Mercedes Benz, it's because they see life where there was death. It wasn't about what I could say to them, preach or tell them. It was about them being able to see me, who was once dead, now alive. It is about them being able to recognize that there is a light in me that wasn't there before. Maybe that would spark some kind of hope in them which is really all that anyone can ask. That was another lesson, but I believe the God was trying to tell me all those years that you kept giving up. All you had to do was just give me a chance. Try me and let me show you that I will help you get through this, learn from it, and then help somebody else. I held onto these things, and I shared them, every chance that I got. When I went through other issues, I used these things to remind me of who God was and to remind me of where I've been. One of the greatest things that I was able to overcome was issues concerning my mom's death. My mother had passed in 1981, and I haven't been back to that cemetery since. My mother's death has always been a source of great pain. I used it to get high, drunk, run away, and hide for years, but now I was healing. Now I was trying to grow. I was trying to look at myself and look at some things in my life. I tried to get through it, but I haven't dealt with my mother's death seriously. I believe the easiest way to start was to actually go to her grave site. My mother was buried in Roosevelt Cemetery in Chesapeake. When I was married, there have been times I have gone down to Portsmouth, but I always found an excuse not to go to my mom's grave. Either I had to get back on time, didn't have enough gas or was too tired or I didn't feel good. This time I made an effort. When I went home to Portsmouth with Jackie, we did my normal routine. We went to Cavalier Manor to see some of the places that I loved and sometimes we would stop by a friend or two to say hi.

We'd go to Mama Chan's to get some sausage and rice and maybe hang out in Chesapeake or Virginia Beach. The plan was to visit my mother's grave on Sunday on our way out. All went according to plan, but when Sunday came along, I was starting to feel really tired. I knew I had to drive, and I wanted to get back to Richmond, so I told Jackie, "Let's hurry up and go. We need to get back in time."

Jackie said," No sir! You're not going to do that this time!"

I just looked at her and I guess I really needed somebody to give me that encouragement. I needed somebody to tell me no. I needed somebody to push me. I'm not saying that I didn't have people in my past that didn't have a desire to push me, but at that time, I really didn't want to be pushed. We found our way to Roosevelt Memorial Cemetery. Now, this is sometime in 2015 and I haven't been there since 1981. I had no idea where my mother's grave site was located. We got out the car next to the main building and I called my aunt Ruth. I explained to her what I was doing and where I was going and how important this was to me. She talked to me over the phone and she kind of guided me on where to go.

She said, "Baby go over to the tree and make a left. Keep going till you see little house or something."

I walked and searched for a while, and then I looked down and I happen to see my mother's grave.

I said, "Okay, Aunt Ruth. I got it.!"

I hung up the phone, sat down and had a little talk and a little cry with my mom. I remember looking up and seeing Jackie videotaping me. I had to apologize to my mom for taking so long to come see her. I apologized to her for being such a bad son. I said that I was sorry for some of the stuff she had to see and for some of the things that I've done. I hope that she forgave me and that she sees that I am trying to do better, although I'm not perfect. I stayed there for about an hour and a half. It felt like a great weight was lifted off me that day. I was no longer held in bondage to my mother's death. Yes, the pain of her death still remains with me, but it doesn't hold me captive anymore.

On one occasion I had the opportunity to speak at an outdoor event in Suffolk. I was invited to come speak by a lady who put the event together. The event was directed towards Health and Wellness and she asked if I wouldn't mind sharing my story. I accepted and on the day of the event, I looked around and I saw all the people at the event having fun. I looked around and I realized that I was in Suffolk, Virginia. I was in prison when my father died, and my aunt had buried him in the Veterans Cemetery in Suffolk. I Googled it and I found out that it was only 10 minutes away. So, while I was speaking, I had an opportunity to incorporate the relationship that I had with my father into the message. I shared that with the group at the end of my message. I told them that I was going to see my father who was 10 minutes away and everybody clapped, because they understood the magnitude of how important that was for me. When I left the event, I went to the cemetery. I was able to find my father's grave and I sat down and talked to him. I didn't really know what to say. I had a lot of issues with my father and many times I hated my father. I blamed my father for my mother's death on more than one occasion. I even blamed my father for my demise on many occasions, but when I looked around, I saw the beauty and elegance of how this Veteran's Cemetery was kept. It let me know that my father did serve his country. My father did die with honor. My father was a Veteran of the United States Army and that made me proud. I went home that day with a little more peace.

So, all in all, life is trying to come back to me, school is still going well, and I am about to graduate. My graduation is a big thing for me because I have never completed anything in my life. I made a serious effort to be able to complete school and receive my degree. It was 2017, and graduation was coming up. I already received a Substance Abuse Counseling Certificate a couple of years ago. On May 14$^{th}$, I was going to receive an associate degree in Human Services. Yes, this was a big deal for me, regardless if it wasn't UVA or Virginia Tech. It was a community college. It was one of the other things that some people said that I would never be able to accomplish or experience. I was told I would never have a driver's license or car. I was told I would be just like my father, and that I would never get a college degree. I wasn't supposed to have meaningful employment.

All of those things turned out to be a lie, because I chose not to believe them. So, as the weekend approached for my graduation, let's look at some things that added to its importance for me. My birthday is May 12$^{th}$, which was that Friday, so Jackie and I decided to go close to DC and stay for the weekend then come back on Sunday May 14$^{th}$, for my graduation, which was also Mother's Day. So, we had a beautiful time, and, on that Saturday, we enjoyed the sights of Northern Virginia and then it was Mother's Day. It was May 14th, 2017 and I was about to graduate college. We drove back to Richmond and we went to the Siegel Center. I saw my classmates, and each one of us had on our robes, hats, and smiles. It was Mother's Day and what a joyous occasion. We all lined up in the Siegel Center and we marched out to the cheers and the claps. I have never experienced anything like this, and I was very proud and very scared at the same time because all I kept saying to myself was, why am I here? How did I get here? I couldn't even enjoy the moment because I was so busy questioning my place right now. So, I'm sitting down and I'm watching the ceremony. I'm looking around and I see family members, children, old people, young people, and handicapped people. Everybody is crossing the stage and then it was my turn.

He said, "Clinton Dukes, Junior!"

I walked across the stage and I received my associate degree on Mother's Day with honors, two days after my birthday. I cannot tell you the sense of pride that I felt that day. I can tell you that regardless of what life has put in your past and regardless of the circumstances, you gender, race, economic, political, or social status; you can always heal. You can always grow if you are willing to look at who you are. I just wished that my mother was here to see it, but somehow, I think she did. A few years have transpired since my graduation and today I have peace, but my peace does not come from the knowledge of knowing that there's no fault in my life. The peace comes from knowing that there is a God that loves me and that he has forgiven me. He has also given me the opportunity to use my pain to help someone else. I would ask God on many occasions and say, Lord you have healed me from many afflictions and much pain, but why do I still carry this pain about my mom's death.

I believe God told me, because you have to keep that. You have to keep that to remind you of where you came from. You have to keep that because it is your greatest tool, but if you use that tool to help others, I will give you peace. I said deal, because all I ever wanted in my life was peace. I always sought it in the wrong things. I sought it in crack pipes, bottles, or between a woman's legs. I thought peace was about the things that I could do, but it was always an inside job. Today I realized what gives me peace. I love to volunteer and share my story. I have an opportunity to go to recovery facilities, schools, and prisons. I used to struggle with how I was going to share in each one, but I had to learn overtime, just tell your story the way you tell your story. People have always embraced it because I was open about it. I also love Marvel movies, because in my past, Spiderman was a big part of my peace that I had when I was a child. When my family life was in turmoil, I could always turn to Spiderman. Today I have opportunities to put on a Spiderman suit, give away toys and take some pictures with kids. On some occasions, give them a message of encouragement. That gives me joy and peace. Some people can't understand why a 50 plus year old man would want to put on the Spiderman costume. Why every time a Marvel movie comes out, I have to be there? Well, I'll tell you. It makes me happy. I'm not drinking or sleeping under a bridge. I'm at peace. I'm not in prison or jail. I work hard and pay my taxes. I volunteer in my community and I'm reliable today. So, I hope you don't mind if I want to be Spiderman on occasion, but all of this can be lost if I don't check myself. One of the most honest things someone has ever told me was that I'm not always honest. Let me say that again. Honestly, I'm not always honest. If you can admit that you have a shot, take it and you will be fine. For a person who's been afflicted with the disease alcoholism and drug addiction, selfishness and self-centeredness are the root of those issues. For me to admit to someone that I'm not always honest is a big deal. It takes me from being selfish to being selfless and that gives me a chance as long as I can admit my faults. As long as I can admit when I'm wrong and not be content to stay there. You must also have the courage to move on. I don't dot every "I" and I don't always cross every "T", but one thing I do believe is that I'm better today than I was yesterday, and I move forward.

I'm trying to become a better person. So, I challenge you today if you have a past similar to mine. You have a choice on how you use it. Your past can either be a stumbling block where you continue to fall over and over again, or you use your past as a steppingstone. Use it to build upon. Instead of allowing your past to become a hindrance choose not to allow yourself to be defined by your circumstances and your situations. Choose not to be defined by what you used to do or be, because what you used to do is not who you are. It's just what you used to do. When we look at people coming out of prison and the people who were enslaved years ago, there's a life-saving lesson to learn. They both had to and they both had to learn how to live free. Many of us want to do better, and many of us do not want to go back to prison, sleep under bridges, or be absent fathers or husbands. We want to be productive members of society, but we have to learn how to live free and sometimes that means taking suggestions from people that we might not want to listen too. Sometimes that might mean humbling yourself and associate with people who you might not normally associated with. What it all boils down to is for you to maintain peace. The process of coming *Out of Egypt is* a great one. There's great joy and happiness coming *Out of Egypt*, but just because you are no longer in Egypt does not mean life is not going to show up. Bills are still going to have to be paid. People are still going to get on your nerves. Tragic situations are going to happen, but you do not have to go back to *Egypt*. You do not have to go back to the streets, prison, or crack houses, but one thing you can do is to give yourself an opportunity to allow God to show you who he is in it. You might not overcome your adversity today, but all you have to do is focus on getting through today. Never allow anyone to steal your joy or your peace today. Life offers many challenges today, but I have not saw the need to drink.

There are many things that could have been said in this book. The wrongs that I have done and the blessings that I have received, but for the protection of myself and others, some of these stories will go to the grave. Some will be shared in different formats. It is my prayer that this book will be a vessel of hope and encouragement for those who have been impacted by various areas of bondage in their lives. We can overcome anything if we are willing to work for it. I don't always smile, do the right thing, go where I'm supposed to go or say what I am supposed to say, but regardless of how tough the issues get sometimes, one thing I have decided to do is stay *Out of Egypt* yall.

School of Humanities
and Social Sciences

REDSKINS

# REST IN PEACE

**Wayne Davis**

*You will be forever missed!*

*Clinton "Tubby" Dukes, Jr.*

# ABOUT THE AUTHOR

Clinton Dukes is a Group Facilitator and Motivational Speaker who uses his past as a tool to help others in Richmond, Virginia. Born in Portsmouth, Virginia, he was the only child of two alcoholic parents, who were in physical fights daily. The death of his mother was the greatest pain he has ever experienced, and he was forced to live with an alcoholic father whom he hated. It is this pain that he used as an excuse to use drugs and drink alcohol. This usage eventually turned into a life of destruction and abuse. The loss of jobs, love ones and opportunities, were only matched by a life of homelessness and incarceration, but it is also this same pain that he uses to help others today. After facing the demons of his past and dealing with the death of his mother, Mr. Dukes found peace in the midst of many storms. Mr. Dukes created a series of teachings called "*Stay Out of Egypt*" which uses the biblical story of the Israelites coming out of bondage and learning how to live free. Today, Mr. Dukes is a college graduate with a degree in Human Services and has a certificate in Substance Abuse Counseling. He shares his story in prisons, treatment centers, and homeless shelters. Mr. Dukes also uses his love for Marvel Comics to dress up as Spiderman to share motivational messages, bring toys and take pictures for children. Every child should have a smile. It is only by God's grace that I stand today. I do not claim perfection, only progress. Mr. Dukes is currently working on the "Out of Egypt Foundation", which will focus on helping the incarcerated, addicted, homeless and children. There's more to come, but in the meantime, stay *Out of Egypt* yall!

Made in the USA
Middletown, DE
12 October 2022